D0163231

FDR and the Bonus Marchers, 1933-1935

FDR and the Bonus Marchers, 1933-1935

GARY DEAN BEST

PRAEGER

Westport, Connecticut
London

Library of Congress Cataloging-in-Publication Data

Best, Gary Dean.
   FDR and the bonus marchers, 1933-1935 / Gary Dean Best.
      p.   cm.
   Includes bibliographical references and index.
   ISBN 0-275-93715-1 (alk. paper)
      1. Hurricanes—Florida—Florida Keys—History—20th century.
   2. Veterans—Florida—Florida Keys—History—20th century.
   3. Natural disasters—Florida—Florida Keys—History—20th century.
   4. Roosevelt, Franklin D. (Franklin Delano), 1882-1945—Relations
   with veterans.   5. Florida Keys (Fla.)—History.   6. United States.
   Federal Emergency Relief Administration—History.   I. Title.
   F317.M7B46   1992
   975.9′41—dc20   92-1194

British Library Cataloguing in Publication Data is available.

Copyright © 1992 by Gary Dean Best

All rights reserved. No portion of this book may be
reproduced, by any process or technique, without the
express written consent of the publisher.

Library of Congress Catalog Card Number: 92-1194
ISBN: 0-275-93715-1

First published in 1992

Praeger Publishers, 88 Post Road West, Westport, CT 06881
An imprint of Greenwood Publishing Group, Inc.

Printed in the United States of America

The paper used in this book complies with the
Permanent Paper Standard issued by the National
Information Standards Organization (Z39.48-1984).

10 9 8 7 6 5 4 3 2 1

LIBRARY
ALMA COLLEGE
ALMA, MICHIGAN

Copyright Acknowledgments

The author and publisher gratefully acknowledge permission to reprint from the following sources.

Articles from the *Washington Post*, March 24 and 25, 1935. Copyright © 1935, the *Washington Post*. Reprinted with permission.

Editorials "Strange Rehabilitation," *Washington Post*, March 25, 1935, and "After the Tragedy," *Washington Post*, September 7, 1935. Copyright © the *Washington Post*. Reprinted with permission.

Articles from the *Miami Herald*, September 5, 8, 9, 11, and 15, 1935. Reprinted with permission of the *Miami Herald*.

Every reasonable effort has been made to trace the owners of copyrighted materials in this book, but in some instances this has proven impossible. The author and publisher will be glad to receive information leading to more complete acknowledgments in subsequent printings of the book and in the meantime extend their apologies for any omissions.

In loving memory
of
Wyatt Dean Bassett
and
Emma Holokahiki Brooks

Contents

Photographs follow p. 100.

Preface

This is primarily an oral and documentary account of a tragedy in the Florida Keys. On Labor Day, September 2, 1935, an incredibly violent hurricane and accompanying tidal wave struck the Florida Keys. Directly in the path of the hurricane were three veterans rehabilitation camps to which some seven hundred World War I veteran "bonus marchers" had been shunted from Washington, D.C., by the Roosevelt administration.

Fortunately, it was immediately after payday for the veterans and many of them were away from the camps in Miami and Key West on furlough. For the approximately four hundred who remained in the camps, September 2, 1935, would be a nightmare that the majority would not survive. By the federal government's count at least 256 veterans lost their lives on that day. The actual total may have been considerably higher. Many more were badly injured. Few survived the tempest unscathed.

The Federal Emergency Relief Administration (FERA), which was responsible for the veterans' presence on the keys, considered the loss of life the result of an "act of God." No one in the FERA or in the Florida ERA, which was responsible for administering the camps, was to blame for the disaster. Roosevelt biographers and New Deal historians have managed to avoid mention of the incident altogether. The veterans who died there have been invisible in the histories for over a half-century.

Materials concerning the tragedy can be found in two record groups of the National Archives and Records Administration. Record Group 69 006.1 of the National Archives contains the FERA documents relating to the hurricane, while Record Group 15, Subgroup 5-3 of the Washington National Records Center contains the Veterans Administration files. Investigations by these two agencies reached very different conclusions concerning the culpability of the officials responsible for the safety of the veterans and both record groups must be consulted to get a reasonably complete picture of the circumstances in the camps that weekend. Unfortunately, some of the documents referred to in the correspondence contained in those files were apparently misplaced or destroyed.

As always I am greatly indebted to the staff of the library of the University of Hawaii at Hilo for their assistance, but in this case I owe a special debt to Kenneth Herrick, director of the library, for obtaining the FERA files for me from the National Archives on microfilm. My wife Lani was, as usual, my inspiration, but she was also of enormous assistance in photocopying and taking notes at the Washington Records Center, in proofreading the final draft of the manuscript, and in helping me with the index. Finally, I want to express my gratitude to the history editor at Praeger, Dan Eades, for his interest and encouragement.

Introduction

It is virtually impossible to escape the story of the bonus marcher episode under President Herbert Hoover in the summer of 1932. Scarcely a month goes by without at least one cable television channel offering a documentary on the 1930s that includes footage of General Douglas MacArthur leading U.S. Army troops against the veterans, driving the bonus expeditionary force from their makeshift camps in Anacostia. No American history textbook would be complete without a description of it. Every biographer of Franklin Delano Roosevelt, Hoover's successor, feels compelled to mention it. Even a short essay by Richard Kirkendall on the New Deal and politics manages to devote a half-page to it.[1] Although no veterans were killed in the incident, it is undoubtedly one of the best-known episodes in twentieth-century American history.

If one is to judge from those same history texts and films, the bonus marchers subsequently exited from American history until the veterans were granted their bonus payments by Congress and the Roosevelt administration in 1936. In short, after the episode of 1932, the bonus marchers became invisible in the histories. In his 1990 biography of Roosevelt, Frank Freidel does not mention them at all after the 1932 incident. A curious student of history might wonder what happened to the bonus movement after 1932. Did the bonus marchers melt away? Were they no longer desirous of the immediate payment of their bonus? Or were they so inspired by the presidential leadership of Franklin D. Roosevelt that they waited passively for the day in 1936 when they received their bonus?

None of these was the case. Several hundred bonus marchers, in fact, descended on Washington in the early weeks of the Roosevelt administration for a convention of the National Veterans' Liaison Committee, called to again apply pressure on the federal government for payment of the bonus. As veterans drifted into the city, they received a very different reception from the Roosevelt administration than they had from its predecessor.

Provisions were first made for feeding and lodging the veterans at Fort Hunt, Virginia. While there, they received a visit from the First Lady, Eleanor Roosevelt, and their leaders were given a cordial reception at the White House by Roosevelt himself. The presence of the veterans so close to the nation's capital could not, however, be allowed to continue lest an incident develop such as that which had so blackened Hoover's reputation. Therefore, the Roosevelt administration offered the veterans work in the Civilian Conservation Corps (CCC) at one dollar a day plus food, clothing, and shelter. After some initial complaints at the low pay, most of the veterans accepted the offer, the others being provided transportation back to their homes by the federal government. By June 1933, some 2,600 veterans had accepted the offer, with another 350 having turned it down.[2] Veterans arriving in the capital in subsequent months were offered the same choice.

Observers of Roosevelt's handling of what might have developed into a difficult problem were impressed. The *Washington Evening Star* wrote that Roosevelt had "followed a policy in dealing with the bonus seekers that by its sincerity and fairness has left them completely disarmed." The *Detroit Free Press* found in Roosevelt's actions proof "of the President's talent for dealing with refractory human beings."[3] The bonus marchers now disappeared from history, invisible amidst the thousands of others who toiled in CCC and FERA camps.

Arthur Schlesinger, Jr., has found in Roosevelt's handling of the bonus marchers a "striking contrast" with Hoover. Not only were the veterans better treated, they were even serenaded by the Navy band. The Roosevelt tactic, Schlesinger has written, was "to kill by kindness."[4] It was an interesting choice of words to describe the fate of the veterans under the Roosevelt administration. In September 1935 Ernest Hemingway wrote of the consequences of that policy for over 250 veterans: "You're dead now, brother, but who left you there in the hurricane months on the Keys where a thousand men died before you in the months when they were building the road that's now washed out? Who left you there? And what's the punishment for manslaughter now?"[5]

Chapter 1

The Invisible

During the first year and a half of the Roosevelt administration, transient veterans showing up in Washington, D.C.,
were offered employment in the Civilian Conservation
Corps (CCC). By August 1935, over eight thousand transient veterans had been enrolled in the CCC. Beginning in
October 1934, transient veterans were also sent to rehabilitation camps in Florida and South Carolina by the Federal
Emergency Relief Administration (FERA) under Harry L.
Hopkins. Between October 12, 1934, and August 9, 1935, a
total of 4,274 transient veterans were employed in these
camps, 2,724 of them in the state of Florida. Establishment
of the camps was recommended by FERA Administrator
Hopkins and approved by President Roosevelt.[1]

In October 1934, the Florida ERA announced that it
would shortly begin to cooperate with the State Road Department on work to close one of the gaps in the projected
overseas highway between the Florida mainland and Key
West, which at that time had been connected only by railroad. A group of some three hundred veterans, recently
brought down from Washington, would begin work late
that month, under the direction of Road Department engineers, on the construction of 4 miles of bridges and 8 miles

of road that would eliminate some 25 miles of ferry jumps. All told, some 30 additional miles would be added to the 90-mile highway that reached from Miami to this point. The announcement also said that a "mobile transient camp" would be erected for the veterans in the keys to house them. It added that the veterans had become available for this project because of delays in a project to restore Fort Jefferson, on Dry Tortugas Island, where they originally were to have been sent.[2]

In December 1934 an inspection was made of the first camp established in the keys. The assistant regional engineer of the FERA, F. C. Boyer wrote:

The Veterans' Rehabilitation Camp at Islamorada is one of several existing or proposed camps to be utilized in the construction of the Over-Seas highway south from Lower Matecumbe to eliminate the northerly of the two gaps in the highway to Key West. This is one of three projects that are to be undertaken under the supervision of Mr. B. M. Duncan, formerly Administrator of Key West. Assisting Mr. Duncan are R. L. Bow, Construction Engineer, and Colonel G. St.C. Robinson, Camp Superintendent.

The camp is located on the S.E. side of Florida Highway 4-A, 2.5 miles north of the Islamorada Station, and covers a tract about one thousand feet parallel with the highway and sloping back approximately four hundred feet to the ocean, giving adequate draining for storm water which promptly soaks into the porous soil or runs off. . . . The operations upon which the men are engaged comprise a quarry three quarters of a mile north of the camp and a construction camp about twelve miles south, at Lower Matecumbe, from which the Over-Seas Highway starts.

The first contingent, of approximately two hundred and fifty men, was quartered at this camp, which was opened by the State Transient Service early in November, and the accommodations existing at the date of this report consisted of sufficient sixteen-foot tents with board floors and siding and with screens and electric lights, each accommodating eight men. In addition, there are a canteen of similar construction, two tents used as an infirmary and dispensary, a frame building for field office and tool room, a similar building for mess hall and kitchen, also one for vegetable storage, a power house, an unscreened latrine and a two-story frame building used as an office and quarters for some of the staff.

Drinking water has to be transported in tank cars from Homestead about fifty miles north on the mainland. For the purpose of insuring an adequate supply of this water, two water towers are under erection, one nearly completed, and a gasoline-driven pump to pump this water from the tank cars on the siding about two hundred feet distant. . . .

On December 19th, a second contingent of approximately two hundred and fifty men arrived. Additional sixteen foot tents, without floors or siding, had been erected to accommodate half of these men. It had been planned to house the remainder of them in box cars pending the erection of more permanent shelter. This was found impractical on the basis of cost, so three large tents, housing forty men each, were secured from Miami and delivered about four o'clock that afternoon. As adequate cots and bedding were available all the men were comfortably sheltered the same night. A urinal was installed at that end of the camp.

The camp being upon the highway, a dangerous condition exists on account of traffic, and the present camp is considered as temporary. When the construction at Lower Matecumbe is completed (at present this camp site is being cleared and the mess hall is in the course of erection) about three hundred men, probably including all those of the second contingent and some of the first, will be transferred there and work will be started on another permanent camp nearer the quarry and at some distance back from the highway. . . .

As tents are claimed not to be satisfactory for all-year use in that locality, the new permanent camps will be of frame construction. The men's quarters will accommodate eight men each in houses 10 ft. by 18 ft., with doorway and three or four windows in each. These, together with mess hall and kitchen, recreation building, offices, staff quarters, store houses and necessary facilities for electricity, water, bathing and toilets, will constitute a camp.

It is intended that the permanent camps will not be occupied until they are fully completed with all facilities available so as to avoid the difficulties and criticisms accompanying the occupation of the first camp.[3]

From this reporting the slap-dash creation and conditions of the camps is clear. The men had been sent down to the keys without adequate preparation having been made for them, as to either accommodations or sanitary provisions.

Another inspection two months later, in late February, was critical of conditions in the camps. Joseph Hyde Pratt, regional engineer for the FERA, reported:

While Camp No. 1, Islamorada, is in much better condition than Camp No. 3, Lower Matecumbe, both of these camps are in a very unsatisfactory condition. Both camps have been planned and constructed without any reference to the Engineering Department of the State ERA. All the work has been done under the supervision of the engineers of the State Road Commission, who planned the camps and have appointed the camp attendants, foremen of the various jobs, without approval of or even reference to the Engineering Department of the State ERA.

Supervisors, foremen, and skilled laborers have been employed from the outside to the extent of a payroll of $5000 per month, and a considerable number of those have been at work on the Works Project (Bridge) and are being paid out of the Florida ERA funds. The veterans are able to furnish a considerable number of men capable of filling these positions, and as FERA is furnishing the funds, meeting the payroll, just as many as possible of these positions should be filled by the veterans. Also the Engineering Department of the Florida ERA should be responsible for the construction of the camp.

Camp No. 1 is a canvas camp, but it is being partly converted into a camp of huts, which at 16' × 10' are to accommodate eight men. Double deck beds are being used.

Camp No. 3 is being converted as rapidly as possible into a hut camp. Men are arriving at these two camps, particularly Camp No. 3, in such large numbers that the camps have not been put in the condition that they should have been before the arrival of the veterans.

The camps should have been put in first class condition before beginning any work on the Bridge Project, unless there were enough veterans to carry out both. The sanitary conditions of the camps should have been the first consideration, and men should have been kept at this work, building toilets and bath houses, sewer lines, and water lines. At present, the sanitary conditions at Camp No. 3 are very bad, as the sewer line has not been constructed nor the toilet houses completed. This camp is not clean; and is badly policed.[4]

Attached to the report was the result of an inspection by the head of the Safety Section of the Florida ERA, Fred B. Ghent, who added the observation that conditions at Camp 1 were "fairly good except for the location of the latrine. The prevailing winds on the lower east coast of the peninsula are from the southeast and the latrine has been located to the windward side of the camp." As for Camp 3, it was described as "very bad," with "cots in the huts placed on the ground, bed linen dirty, men [having] to walk around in the sand which is the floor of their quarters." The safety inspector recommended: "In view of the fact that the supervision of the construction of this job is furnished by the State Road Department, it is recommended and requested that a full-time safety inspector from our Organization be placed at this location for the protection of the men from the veterans' camp."[5]

Clearly, in its rush to rid Washington of the potentially troublesome veterans, the Roosevelt administration had not given, and was not even now giving, consideration to the conditions under which the veterans were being housed and cared for on the keys. The Florida Road Department clearly put its priority on the construction of the Overseas Bridge Project and was content to allow the veterans to live under the conditions of a temporary transient camp. Had it not been for the intervention of the Florida State Emergency Relief Administration (ERA), that priority would probably have continued and it is doubtful that conditions in the camps would have improved even to the limited extent that they did.

Upon receiving the reports from Pratt and Ghent, the assistant administrator of the Florida ERA wrote to B. M. Duncan, the state road engineer in charge of the Overseas Bridge Project and, therefore, of the camps as well, telling Duncan:

The Director of our Safety Department made a report to the Administration under date of February 25th on insanitary [sic] conditions existing at the Veterans' Rural Rehabilitation Camps. In this same report he brought to our attention several dangerous conditions which obtain in the construction work being carried on at Lower Matecumbe. . . .

It is the desire of the [Florida Emergency Relief] Administration that the premises and quarters of the camps in which the veterans are living be kept in the most sanitary condition possible and that every precaution be maintained to insure the safety of the men working on the construction projects. The attention of those individuals specifically in charge of the camps and construction work should be given to the welfare and safety of these veterans.[6]

Soon after these visits, in late February 1935, the veterans' camps broke briefly into the news when the erstwhile bonus marchers went on "strike" at the camp located on Lower Matecumbe Key. A letter from six of the leaders of the strike to the administrator of the bridge project complained that the veterans had been told the project was originated for the benefit of the veterans, but in actuality they were not being given work that was in accord with their qualifications. A number of higher-salaried outside workers had been hired to do work that the veterans were qualified to do, but the veterans had not been given an op-

portunity to apply for the positions. The "civilian" workers were also getting preference in the mess hall and in the
issue of clothing, and were living "four people to a bunk
house while the veterans are quartered eight to a shack."
In sum, the veterans wanted to be treated the same as the
"civilian" workers. Moreover, the veterans insisted that
priority should be given "to sanitary conditions. With four
hundred men in camp it is self-evident that the present
sanitary conditions are wholly inadequate and unhealthy."
The camps had no electricity, no bathhouses, and water
only for drinking. The mess hall was so inadequate that
many men spent the entire lunch hour lined up to get in.[7]

The National Guard was called in to patrol the area and
prevent veterans from the Lower Matecumbe camp from
enlisting those in other nearby camps to join the strike.
The veterans claimed that they were being held prisoner in
the camp by the guardsmen and denied contact with the
outside world.[8] Efforts on the part of deputy sheriffs to
keep newsmen out of the camp caused a near riot over the
apparent attempt to keep the veterans' side of the story
from reaching the press. The newsmen were allowed to
stay, and described the conditions under which the 425
men of the camp were forced to live. The *Miami Daily
News* wrote:

The men are quartered in 40 bunkhouses, holding eight men
each, 10 tents with four men each, and one large tent with 40
men. They did not have fresh water for bathing, they said, and
must use salt water. They made no complaint of the food, but ob-
jected to the civilian workers being waited on while they stood
in line and washed their dishes.[9]

After a few days, "all quiet" was reported at the Lower
Matecumbe camp, with the veterans having returned to
work after peaceful settlement of their grievances.[10]

The camps on the Florida Keys were located at Islamorada and Lower Matecumbe, remote from any commercial center. The nearest town was Homestead, with a population of about thirty-five hundred, located approximately sixty miles from the camp headquarters. Drinking water was shipped in from Homestead in tank cars.[11]

An unsigned report of a meeting held on March 2 concerning the camps found Duncan instructed "to concentrate the work of the veterans to the completion of the sewer line, and the construction of adequate toilets and bath houses."[12] Another memorandum, written on March 5 by Joseph Hyde Pratt, the regional engineer, suggested that authority over the veterans' camps be divided, with the Overseas Bridge Project directed by the State Road Department, as at present, but the "actual conduct of the camps as distinguished from the work program shall be the responsibility of a state veterans rehabilitation director, who shall be responsible to the state [Florida ERA] administrator." The memorandum added:

A large percentage of these Veterans are problem cases and they do not seem to be able to assume responsibility, but want to be taken care of. Most of them when handled right are willing to work and will work diligently and well. The work of the Veterans, however, should not be the main consideration, but secondary to their welfare. The medical care and supervision of the men is not considered satisfactory and efficient by the Regional Engineer and the doctor in charge is not considered competent. His dismissal has been suggested. Any doctor who would consider the sanitary condition of Camp No. 3 as satisfactory and so state his opinion to newspaper reporters . . . will not make a satisfactory medical attendant for any camp.[13]

Thus, it would appear that the priorities of the several agencies involved in the camps were different. The Florida ERA wanted priority put on the welfare of the veterans; the State of Florida, especially the Road Department, appears to have been more interested in the Overseas Bridge Project. Now the authority over the men in the camps would be divided between the two agencies that reflected the different priorities.

The resulting confusion of authority over the camps is illustrated by the testimony of Conrad Van Hyning, administrator of the Florida ERA after July 1, 1935. The camps, he testified, were under his "general supervision," with Fred Ghent the direct supervisor. When asked if the camps were a state project or a federal project, Van Hyning thought that "technically it was a state project." Asked if the federal government had "issued any instructions to you as to how these camps would be operated," Van Hyning denied that he had received "what might be called definite intructions." He added:

The instructions issued were that the men were to be paid $1 a day, the same rate as the CCC camp was getting, to perform a full day's work for services in return for that pay. They were to be treated as civilians rather than—that is, there was not to be an army system—CCC rules did not apply and they were set up as a sort of a cross between a CCC camp and a Transient Camp. The general plan was to approximate the CCC program without giving them the same official status.[14]

News of the strike at Lower Matecumbe Key attracted the attention of the *Washington Post*, a frequent New Deal critic, to the Florida veterans' work camps. In late March, Edward T. Folliard began a series of articles on the camps. He found them recovering from a recent "booze rampage" and living in "a comparative paradise—a palm-dotted strand, washed by the blue-green waters of the Atlantic and the Gulf of Mexico and caressed at this time by a delightful breeze from the East." Here they were eating "three whopping meals a day" and received wages ranging from thirty to forty dollars per month. Folliard wrote:

In a sense it is a transplanted bonus camp. The veterans drift into Washington and from there they are sent down here to Florida or to somewhat similar camps in South Carolina. The Federal

Emergency Relief Administration foots the bill. . . . Thus far 1,900 veterans have been sent South to be rehabilitated.

Folliard found that the National Guard was still patrolling the camps, many of them also on relief. He wrote:

They have a most unusual tactical problem. It is to keep bootleggers away from the veterans. No bootleggers were visible hereabouts today. Neither was the "Showboat" to be seen. This boat came down from Miami, loaded with women. They left with a lot of FERA money. Some other women came here from Miami, 74 miles away, and Key West, 82 miles away, by automobile. They, too, took away chunks of FERA cash.

All of this had happened during a three-day drunk that had begun on payday, during which time most of the veterans had refused to work.[15]

Despite their balmy tropical location and a life of comparative ease that included menus like hot cakes and bacon for breakfast, veal cutlets with brown gravy for lunch, and braised beef and mashed potatoes for dinner, the veterans, Folliard found, would gladly give it up if paid their bonus. If the bonus were paid, he concluded, most of the veterans would be gone by the next day. He wrote: "They concede that the Florida Keys are enchanting, that the food is even better than in the army and that the pay is 'pretty fair,' but none of these things would hold them here if a bonus of $600 or $700 came along."[16] Two months later Roosevelt vetoed the bonus bill which had been passed by Congress. The veterans, who might have left if the bonus bill had become law, remained in the camps.

The *Post* responded to its reporter's account of the camps with an editorial, in which it wrote:

The accounts of conditions in the Florida veterans' camps visited by a *Post* correspondent will shock even the most hard-boiled observers. Descriptions of drunkenness and debauchery at the expense of, and in effect under the auspices of, the Federal Government are enough to discourage the most ardent advocates of special camps for former doughboys. While it is obviously unfair to generalize from such scandalous examples of emergency mal-administration, the FERA is certainly on the defensive so far as its "relief" policy for veterans is concerned.

Conditions in the Florida camps raise the question of why such special treatment for veterans was ever ordered in the first place. The beneficiaries—or victims—of this policy are principally veterans who were evicted from the Washington bonus camps in 1932. Instead of being granted relief along with other transients they now bask beneath the palms of the South Atlantic. The more enterprising, it is reported, save their "pay" of a dollar a day and take occasional trips back to Washington, where they ultimately report to relief headquarters for return rides to their southern base.

Of all possible ways to encourage discontent, none could surpass this scheme of herding dissatisfied men together on an island with food, lodging and cash to buy liquor provided.[17]

One difficulty with the camps was apparent confusion over who was in charge. In mid-March, Julius F. Stone, Florida ERA administrator, wrote B. M. Duncan to confirm the arrangements that had been made for separate administration of the work and the camps. He wrote:

The whole program, administratively, will be divided into two divisions: Camp Division and Work Division. You will direct the Work Division and Mr. Hinchman will direct the Camp Division. The Work Division will have jurisdiction over all matters pertaining to the conduct of the actual work project; whereas, the Camp Division will have jurisdiction over all matters other than those which are the responsibility of the Work Division.[18]

Hinchman, however, remained for only a couple of weeks and was ultimately replaced by Ray W. Sheldon in charge of the camps on the Keys, under the direct authority of Fred B. Ghent, the former FERA safety director, who now became director of the veterans' camps. The result of the new organization plan was not only to divide authority over the veterans, but to create entirely different chains of command up the line from the two on-site administrators.

Lorin Scott, the chief clerk in charge of the camp's routine office work until late May, complained that it was never clear whether the camps were under the jurisdiction of Florida state authorities or the FERA headquarters in Washington and that when the men were at work they were apparently under another authority. People wandered in and out of the office claiming authority, but there was no clearly defined organizational chart or chain of command. Then, in March, Fred Ghent, formerly state safety director, appeared on the scene, told the veterans that he had been placed in charge of the ten camps in Florida, stayed about three weeks, and then, in the words of the chief clerk, "pulled out for Miami. At no time was anybody there officially notified of any change in directorship in an executive capacity. However, he did leave men in charge who were signing such notes and bulletins as were necessary, usually . . . with the title of 'Acting Assistant Director.'" Frustrated at his inability to get decisions made, Scott resigned on May 21. When asked who Ghent had left in charge of the camps, the chief clerk responded: "So many that I could hardly keep up with them, right there in the office with them; I could not possibly remember them in their sequence." The men, he stated, were not qualified for the job: "They lacked any background of experience, either in the conduct of the Camps or the carrying on of the project, that is, the operations." Of Ghent, he said:

Mr. Ghent was, I think, one of those peculiar men who could not make up his mind. . . . [H]e was not a vicious man, but just could not make up his mind to anything. I think he was a poor executive to head a job of any kind—the poorest that I have ever seen in forty-three years of experience, and I have seen quite a few. . . . He could not even make up his mind whether he wanted to pay a man $45 per month or $36 per month. He just couldn't make up his mind to anything.[19]

Ghent's appointment had apparently been dictated by the FERA in Washington.[20]

A veteran at Camp 1, one of "the first ten" to inhabit the camp, testified:

I do know this, that we were about four or five months there at #1, we built the camp, we never even had bathing facilities; I do know the sanitary conditions of the camp were almost—well, I couldn't understand; there were flies, you go in to eat there would be flies, you would have to fan them out of your face and food; finally they eliminated that. . . . And a lot of time we didn't see but one person that ever represented any religious organization, that was Father McDonald from Homestead. We didn't even have as much as a book or a movie—moving pictures—so when they started to give them a dollar a day they would get trucks and take you to Tavernier to a picture show. And we were supposed to have had a recreation hall at #1, but never did get it. They were starting it before we left. And the men, as far as I could see, in my view of the whole thing, it was practically the men were left just to do any old way, that was all; there was no rules or regulations when we first went there, and there never was. No one knew anything; when we were building the road I asked some of the men in charge and they couldn't tell me anything. I saw stuff in the roads—sheets, pillowcases, blankets, beds. There was a tool house, when we turned in the tools, not even locked up; if you wanted an axe or pick or saw, just walk in and get it, when we first went there. After making some changes they finally got a few rules, but was never any known regulations. And they would discharge the men and send them to Washington, and the same men would come back again; I have known men who went to Washington two or three times, the government would pay their way and they would hobo back to Washington and they would send them back again. I guess some of those men had their fare paid two or three times by the United States government. . . . So the only thing that I can see, as far as the sociology part of the camp is concerned, was the matter of fact that the people who hit camp at first, we never had any rules or regulations, and it just got off on the wrong foot, someway or other. But we had a strike down there; they told us in Washington we were the same as the CC's (Civilian Conservation Corps), and so they wanted to work six days a week, two shifts; so the men said well we are supposed to work the same as the CC. And they all struck, and they ran the first sergeant out. . . . I was in charge of the infirmary there for four or five months, starting off, when we built the camp. I think if we had had more recreation there it would have been better for the men, but they didn't get it; I don't know whether the money was about through, or what, but that was one thing I noticed was lacking.[21]

Early in April, Ghent wrote to Colonel Joseph Hyde Pratt, of the FERA:

We have certain obstacles to overcome and hazards which we have to recognize in connection with the Veterans Rehabilitation Program in this area.

As I understand it, we expect to have between 1500 and 2000 veterans encamped on the Keys by the first of July. There will also be several hundred civilian employees used in connection with construction projects. The hurricane season begins July 1st and continues through the last full moon in October. It has been known that during this period of the year no hurricane approached the proximity of the Keys. We do know, however, that this area is subject to hurricanes, and in view of this knowledge, it is our duty to every man employed on the Keys in connection with this program to furnish a safe refuge during a storm.

Ghent suggested that a large warehouse be constructed with facilities for accommodating the men on the second floor, well-located, built in such a way as to be able to with-stand winds, and high enough above ground to escape flooding. Alternatively, Ghent suggested that arrangements be made with the Florida East Coast Railway "to keep on hand at Miami sufficient equipment to move the entire number of men off the Keys when we get a report that a hurricane is approaching our location." Ghent had discussed the alternatives with B. M. Duncan, engineer in charge of the bridge work, and Duncan leaned toward the railroad alternative.[22] After the hurricane Ghent testified that he had received no answer from the FERA to this letter.[23] No warehouse was built because of the expense that would have been involved. Nor were any definite arrangements made with the Florida East Coast Railway for evacuating the veterans in the event of an emergency because, Ghent testified, "of the unsettled conditions of the Veterans Work Program, and the absence of any instructions [from Washington] as to how the program should be run."[24]

Late in July, Van Hyning traveled to Washington with Fred Ghent

to arrange for the transfer of these camps to the CCC. We felt that the bridge had not turned out to be a practical project for their work on the Keys [and] the camp situation wasn't satisfactory. The camps themselves didn't provide sufficient recreational facilities and a normal outlet for the men and to make these things available was to[o] expens[iv]e and they would be happier in the CCC camps. The whole general plan was not particularly satisfactory, and we were told by FERA Washington that a transfer would be made to the CCC, and they would get in touch with the proper officials and try to arrange a transfer within the next month.

Asked if he knew who had appointed Ghent director of the camps, Van Hyning answered: "It was my understanding that he was selected by one of the representatives of the FERA in Washington, a special representative for the camps." Van Hyning added of Ghent, "I did not feel that he was a satisfactory man for the job. If the camps had gone on, he knew he was to go out and it didn't seem that there was any use in hiring a new director."²⁵

In August the *New York Times* discovered the veterans' camps. One of its reporters, Charles McLean, visited a camp near Charleston, South Carolina, and wrote:

A war veterans' heaven, fostered by the fear of the [Roosevelt] administration that another "Hoover bonus march" might descend upon Washington, and directed by Harry L. Hopkins, Relief Administrator, has sprung up seven miles from this city. Incidentally, it has created a separate veterans' administration from that managed by General Frank T. Hines. It threatens to grow to such proportions that grave concern is already felt by those in charge.

The camp, situated in three hundred acres of pine forests, housed veterans under conditions that "surpass in comfort those occupied by the majority of army troops." Some 445 bonus marchers had been shipped there by the Roosevelt administration to "keep them from agitating for payment of their certificates." They were paid thirty to forty-five dollars per month, in addition to whatever compensation some were receiving for wartime disabilities. The liquor stores, he reported, did a thriving business every payday.²⁶

Early in August the *New York Times* found about twenty-five hundred veterans in the eleven camps—seven camps in Florida and four in South Carolina, including separate camps for black and white residents. An assistant federal ERA administrator told the newspaper that the camps were a cross between "the Civilian Conservation Corps and a work relief project." The *Times* went on:

They represent President Roosevelt's solution of the "problem" of the transient veteran, which threatened last August to become acute and did become acute in January, when nearly 500 were registered at the transient bureau in the capital.

The question [of] what to do with them was discussed at that time by Mr. Hopkins and Robert L. Fechner, director of the CCC camps, and the President who, according to FERA officials, suggested the Southern camp plan and approved the program worked out by Mr. Hopkins for their establishment and maintenance.

The Veterans Bureau is a participant only to the extent of determining for the local transient bureau whether the registered applicants are in fact veterans. Four thousand such applicants have been certified by Veterans Bureau records since last October [1934], according to A.D. Hiller, executive assistant to Brg. Gen. Frank T. Hines, administrator of veterans' affairs.[27]

Charles McLean, the *New York Times* reporter, did not reach the camps in Florida, but he found plenty in South Carolina that amused him. In Kingstree, South Carolina, he found veterans building a golf course for a town of three thousand people in which almost no one played golf. Moreover, most of the men's time was spent in driving back and forth between the camp and the golf course project. The veterans were so rowdy, he found, that the women of the town drove to other towns and cities to shop on veterans' paydays in order to avoid them in Kingstree's business district. A Baptist minister of the town told him:

I think that it is extremely unfortunate that the government would harbor 250 men of such temperaments, with so much leisure time to foment discontent and dissension among themselves. It is not the fault of the men, but of the government which sent them here.

It is far better that these men be sent back to their homes and there paid $30 a month.[28]

Of the veterans in Blaney, South Carolina, McLean wrote:

When the Federal Emergency Relief Administration took veterans off the streets of Washington to avert another "Hoover Bonus March," the net result as far as it concerns the productive labor of 265 of them concentrated in a camp near here has been the construction for themselves of an "old-fashioned fishing hole."

The men, he wrote, spent most of their time "footing it" to a local beer shack or getting hold of moonshine whiskey, while others spent their money on "brass-ankle women."[29]

Nationally syndicated columnist Raymond Clapper, invariably friendly to the Roosevelt administration, wrote that "those who have wondered why we have had no bonus marches and demonstrations at Washington during the [Roosevelt] Administration" could find the answer in Florida. He explained:

For more than two years it has been the policy to spirit gathering veterans out of Washington and into concentration camps far away from the Capital's spotlight. About a dozen veterans' camps have been maintained, five in Florida and the others in various Southern states where winters are mild. Whenever a group gathered at the transient camp in Washington, Veterans' Bureau officials went among them, offered them free transportation, $30 a month and keep in Florida. Veterans either accepted the offer or vanished to seek transient relief elsewhere.

Some seven hundred of the veterans, he noted, were stationed in three Florida veterans' camps in the keys.[30]

In its August 16, 1935, edition, the *New York Times* reported that Harry L. Hopkins, FERA administrator, had announced that the "FERA camps in the South to which some 3,500 jobless war veterans were quietly sent, partly because of the [Roosevelt] administration's fear of another bonus march," would be closed as of November 1, with the able-bodied veterans transferred to CCC camps or work-relief jobs. The *Times* noted that the announcement that the camps would be closed had come after its publication "of a series of articles revealing their existence and describing conditions in them."[31]

Time magazine took note of the *New York Times* articles in its August 26 edition, and wrote:

If President Hoover had shipped the Bonus Army of 1932 off to pleasant camps to play, putter and carouse at Government expense, the nation's Press would almost certainly have been more indignant than it was at his action in driving the luckless veterans out of Washington with tear gas and bayonets. If the conscientious New York Times had not last fortnight dispatched a man to investigate and report[,] the quiet but costly fashion in which President Roosevelt dissipated the threat of another Bonus Army would probably have escaped all public notice.

Shrewd Franklin Roosevelt never let his bonus marchers get the Washington spotlight. Quick as querulous, down-at-the-heels veterans began shuffling into Washington, he began shipping them off to special relief camps in the South.[32]

After the hurricane, *Time* wrote: "In 1933 another Bonus Army marched on Washington. Instead of routing it with tear gas, resourceful President Roosevelt deployed the disconsolate, down-at-heel veterans into special work camps in South Carolina and Florida." It added:

If the U.S. had a Devil's Island, the Florida Keys would be a good place to locate it. A collection of mangrove swamps and low islands of coral sand, they were hot, humid, alive with mosquitoes, and while rattlesnakes coil in the underbrush, sharks, barracudas and poisonous rays infest the milky water. The veterans started kicking as soon as they got there, cursed the poor food, flimsy houses, inadequate medical care, the militia which was sent to quell their rioting.[33]

In actuality, of course, it appears that the decision to transfer the veterans to the CCC had been made even before the appearance of the *New York Times* article, when Van Hyning and Ghent visited Washington in early August. Clearly, the FERA in Washington had for months pre-

viously lost interest in the veterans it had left exposed on
the Florida Keys during hurricane season. Ghent testified
that the camps had "operated without any definite instructions from the authorities at Washington, since April 1st,
1935." He added:

I have assumed entire responsibility in all matters pertaining to
the Veterans Works Program. The program had grown to such
proportions that I felt that we needed some definite instructions,
and a definite program on which to operate. I went to Washington on August 6th with Mr. Conrad Van Hyning and Mr.
Robert Unkrich [deputy to Van Hyning] and endeavored for
three days and a half to find out something definite—without
any results.

When asked if he had received any instructions from
Washington concerning protection of the veterans against
hurricanes or other storms, Ghent repeated that he had received "no instructions from Washington since April 1st,
pertaining to the Veterans program in Florida." As for spe-
cific steps to be taken in the event of a hurricane, Ghent
testified that he had written "a letter to Colonel Pratt
[southeastern regional engineer for the FERA] at Washington the first of May; I think the date of the letter, to be
exact, is May 4th; outlining some problems which I wanted
Washington to rule on. That letter was never answered by
Colonel Pratt or anyone else from Washington." In that
letter Ghent had "outlined two plans for handling the men
during hurricanes; one was the construction of a storm
refuge, and the other was the movement of the men out of
the area on trains." In this crucial matter, the administrators
of the camps on the Florida Keys were left without guidance
from the New Deal administrators in Washington.[34]

The confusion over authority (symbolized by the FERA
and the Florida ERA), the difference in priorities, and
Washington's indifference to the condition and fate of the

veterans on the Florida Keys seemed unimportant now, for the camps were soon to be closed.

By the middle of August, then, the methods used by the Roosevelt administration to deal with the problem of the bonus marchers had begun to embarrass it, and the camps were to be closed as of November 1, 1935. The camps on the Florida Keys, however, would be closed before that date. Mother Nature would not wait for November 1, and when she struck the camps the confused authority and divided priorities would not serve the veterans in the camps well. After September 1, 1935, the Roosevelt administration would wish either that it had closed the camps a month earlier, or that it had provided for better administration of them.

Chapter 2

The Hurricane

WARNINGS

The *Miami Herald* of September 1, 1935, carried warnings from the weather bureau of tropical storms that might hit the Florida coast. Precise predictions of locations and paths of such storms were difficult in 1935 because most of the monitoring devices available today did not exist then. There were, for example, no "hurricane hunter" aircraft and no weather satellites. The accuracy of weather bureau reports depended on their own sources of information. Where tropical storms and hurricanes were concerned, these depended on reports from the islands experiencing the storms and from ships or planes at sea that encountered them. Hurricanes could grow in intensity and change course over water without the changes being detected unless an unlucky ship or aircraft wandered into their paths. Given the unpredictability of storm behavior in the Caribbean, well-known by those experienced in such matters, the mere existence of a tropical storm in the area was reason for preparations to be made.

The next day's *Herald* contained the news that Havana was preparing for the hurricane, with the headline

"Cubans Fleeing As Storm Nears." The weather bureau was reporting that the hurricane would "probably strike the Florida channel." On September 3 the *Herald* reported that the storm was "centered over the extreme southwestern tip of the mainland," and that an "11-car Florida East Coast Railway train left Miami at 4:30 P.M. Monday for Matecumbe to evacuate more than 500 world war veterans encamped there." All veterans were to be evacuated to Hollywood, Florida. But as of 11:30 P.M., September 2, railway officials had reported that "they had received no word from the special train sent to Matecumbe. Their communications system, they said, was disrupted south of Homestead." Stories datelined September 2 reported that officials of the veterans' camps were making arrangements with the city manager of Hollywood, Florida, to house the veterans there temporarily. All these efforts were too late. The veterans were not evacuated. They did not arrive in Hollywood.

The veterans' camps were located on keys barely above sea level, with scant natural protection against high winds or waves. Priority having been given to work on the Overseas Bridge Project, only flimsy shacks had been erected to house and feed the men and these offered no manmade protection against the same elements. It should have been evident that even a mild tropical storm or the weaker fringes of a hurricane could have a lethal effect in such circumstances. As Walter J. Bennett, the senior meteorologist at Jacksonville, later pointed out, even if the hurricane had pased through the Florida straits rather than hitting the keys, it "would have caused high tides, and strong gales on the Florida Keys, with tides possibly as high, but not higher than, ten feet above mean low tide, and winds between gale and hurricane force." Such tides and winds, he added, always did "a great deal of damage" to "flimsy buildings."[1] Therefore, the presence of a hurricane in the Caribbean should have inspired preparations no matter what its predicted course, from concern that even the fringes of the storm system could be a danger to the camps.

Since no building had been constructed for the protection of the men, as Ghent had suggested, reliance was instead placed on the Florida East Coast Railway (FEC) to evacuate the men before a storm hit. Two assumptions apparently entered into the calculations of those responsible for the veterans' camps as they prepared for the possibility of a storm on the keys: (1) in a normal working situation, the FEC would be able to put together a special train without undue delay, and (2) a rescue train would be able to proceed to the keys from Miami in the usual length of time required for such a trip. The defects in the latter assumption should have been obvious to those in charge of the camps. If the winds and tides associated with a hurricane were striking the tip of the mainland and the keys, it was unlikely that a train would be able to make the trip in the length of time it took under normal conditions. If those in charge of the camps waited until conditions were such that it was certain the veterans needed to be evacuated, the conditions would also be such as to make evacuation by train extremely risky.

The first assumption also proved wrong in the circumstances. The hurricane did not strike on a normal working day, but over Labor Day weekend when the FEC was operating with only a skeleton crew. Men had to be called in from their weekend leisure to prepare and man the train. With this additional delay, timely notice from those responsible for the camps to the FEC that a train should be prepared was critical for the safety of the veterans. In addition to the dangerous situation in which the veterans had been placed by the priority on bridge construction, by the presence of the tropical storm and by wrong assumptions about the speed with which a rescue train could be obtained, there were also the consequences of the confusion of authority over the camps.

As the storm approached neither Ray W. Sheldon nor Fred Ghent were at the camps. Sheldon, who was in direct charge, was in Key West. On Saturday night he called the Key West Weather Bureau to inquire about the storm, adding that if it looked threatening he intended to return to the camps on the Sunday morning ferry. He was told that as of Saturday night, August 31, conditions did not appear very alarming for the keys. The Weather Bureau promised to call him if conditions changed. At 5:00 A.M. Sunday morning the meteorologist phoned Sheldon to tell him that "our intermediate observations at 2:00 A.M. conditions looked as though the storm might prove dangerous on the Florida Keys; so I advised him to take the early morning ferry and return." He had, he said, tried to convey to Sheldon that there was danger in the area of the veterans camps, that "it was impossible to say just where the storm would strike and just how hard it would strike, but being familiar with hurricanes I thought it would be advisable to take every precaution in advance, and thought he should be on the ground as early as possible." He did not, however, suggest to Sheldon that the camps be evacuated.

Incredibly, the meteorologist also testified that "the veterans camp—that the officials—never requested they be advised from the Key West Weather Bureau office, and they were not on our storm warning list. The only party listed for storm warning information on the upper keys was the State Highway Project headquarters at Lower Matecumbe." Thus, the Work Division was getting reports from the nearest weather station, but not the Camp Division, which was responsible for the safety of the men. On Sunday, September 1, as a result of the new information which had prompted the call to Sheldon, the Weather Bureau ordered the hoisting of storm warnings and notified the State Highway Project headquarters at Lower Matecumbe that they should "take every precaution for a severe storm and secure their equipment." The FEC office was also informed and the warning transmitted to the stations along its line. By Sunday night, September 1, the town of Key West was almost entirely boarded up in readiness for a severe storm. Subsequent observations, however, suggested that the storm would not hit the keys directly, and it was not until the middle of the afternoon on Monday, September 2, that it became obvious that the storm would hit them.[2]

Sheldon called the Miami Weather Bureau on Sunday night and asked if it would be advisable for the men to remain in the camps until Monday morning. Ernest Carson, the meteorologist in charge, could not recall who he had talked to, but testified:

I told them that it would be safe to stay until Monday morning. At 10:30 Monday morning—it was between ten and eleven—he called again, and I gave him these messages about hurricane warnings going up at Key West and he said they were getting out. I thought perhaps the train was there and they could get on the train then. They had plenty of time to get out then.

He was, he added, "surprised they had not already gone."[3] The Miami meteorologist was wrong: the train was not there. The veterans' camps were not ready to be evacuated when the Weather Bureau warned of imminent danger; instead, the warning would be taken as the signal that the train should be ordered, which would delay an evacuation by several additional hours even if the two assumptions about the FEC had been correct.

Carson also testified that in July, over a month before the hurricane, Sam Cutler had visited the weather bureau office to ask about receiving warnings. Carson had told him that the camps were "in the Key West section," but that Miami would "gladly give him a copy of any warnings we had." He also recalled that he had told Cutler "that any time a tropical storm was approaching the Florida straits that they should take precautions." The Miami Weather

Bureau was under the impression, he said, that the camps would be ready to evacuate by train Monday morning.[4] Obviously there was confusion over the location and course of the hurricane during a crucial period of time late Sunday and early Monday, but the presence of the storm, the very confusion over its course, and the likely effects that even the fringes of such a storm would have had on the camps should have dictated greater precautions than those that were taken. The warnings from the Key West meteorologist on Sunday morning would seem to have suggested the desirability of ordering the train then, even before the erroneous conclusion that the storm had changed its course away from the keys.

THE TRAIN

Like many business concerns, the FEC had not fared well during the depression and was in receivership. Scott Loftin, one of the co-receivers, recalled that Ghent had visited him in May 1935 to take "up with me the question of furnishing special trains to move veterans from camps on the Keys, in the event of requests made for the purpose, due to hurricanes." On June 6 Loftin wrote Ghent that "we would be able to furnish locomotives and equipment to make up two trains, and they would be available after receiving twelve hours' notice of his desire for them."[5]

On Sunday morning, at about 6:10 A.M., J. L. Byrum, chief train dispatcher for the FEC, testified that he participated in a telephone conversation with Ghent and another dispatcher. They discussed, Byrum said,

the probability of getting at least four (4) coaches on No. 76 Sunday night for movement of veterans from the Keys, Mr. Ghent explaining that a number of his men would be in either Key West or Miami and there should be somewhere between 200 and 250 to move out in case weather conditions demanded; I explained to him that the only way for me to get the coaches in position would be to forward them from Miami on No. 75 that morning, to return [from Key West] on No. 76, which I would do.

The additional coaches were ordered and returned from Key West that afternoon, together with yet another coach added in Key West "to be sure we had ample coach space for the veterans from the Keys in case it was decided to come out on No. 76." With ten coaches on No. 76, it would have been possible, he said, to carry eight hundred men from the veterans' camps in addition to their regular passengers. He added:

We endeavored several times to ascertain through the agent at Islamorada whether there was a probability of the veterans using the coaches as if we could get definite advice that they were not coming out on No. 76 we would leave one of the extra coaches at Key West; but we were not able to ascertain whether any decision had been made about bringing the men out that night. After the train passed Islamorada the Trick Train Dispatcher ascertained definitely that the veterans did not use the train.[6]

Before Byrum got on the line, Ghent had been talking to E. H. Hall, train dispatcher. According to Hall's recollection of his conversation with Ghent, the latter had been concerned with the cost of adding the additional coaches to Nos. 75 and 76, if they were not actually used by the veterans. Hall "replied that I did not know but my thought was there would not be any charge. In other words, I gave him the impression if we arranged for the movement of the equipment and he used it, we would, of course, collect transportation, but if it were not used there would be no collection."[7]

Despite the efforts of the FEC to accommodate an evacuation of the camps Sunday evening, then, the camp directors had not loaded the men on the enhanced train. The additional cars were left on Nos. 75 and 76 the following day, the day of the hurricane, in case the veterans might want to use them to evacuate on the return train from Key West, which normally left at 5:30 P.M.[8] If the hurricane had held off for as long as Sheldon and Ghent thought it would when they first made the decision to order the special train, a special train would not have been needed; the men could have left on No. 76. But the hurricane did hit, and No. 76 did not leave until early on Tuesday morning, when it could travel only as far north as Marathon, halfway to the camp.[9]

On the night of September 1, Sheldon phoned P. L. Gaddis, district superintendent of the FEC, to ask how long it would take to get a train to the camps to evacuate about four hundred men. Gaddis replied "to the effect that our train had just come in from Key West and that this train was then at the Miami passenger station and that we could arrive there (Islamorada) with this train, with coaches enough to take care of 400 men, in about four hours." Sheldon told him that "he would, when the necessity arose, order a train through his Jacksonville office."[10] As Gaddis recalled the conversation, he was at first under the impression that Sheldon wanted to order the train then, but Sheldon reiterated, "I don't mean now; I will handle it through Jacksonville tomorrow about the train; I just want to know how long it would take to get it down there." According to Gaddis, Sheldon asked again, "About four hours?" And Gaddis replied, "Yes, now, if you order the train now." Asked by investigators if he had indicated to Sheldon that "if he ordered the train tomorrow, Monday, that it would take longer than four hours to get it there," Gaddis indicated that he had not.[11] Sheldon apparently concluded that a train ordered at any time could arrive in four hours.

Thus, the train that had returned from Key West without

the veterans was in the station and ready to make a special trip back to the keys to evacuate them. The reference to Jacksonville meant that the train would be ordered, if necessary, by Ghent. Of note is the fact that Gaddis had indicated to Sheldon that even with a train already made up and still in good weather, it would take four hours to get the train to the camps. That it would take considerably longer if a train were not already made up and had to travel through heavy weather ought to have been obvious to Sheldon, even if Gaddis had not made that explicit.

Having missed two opportunities to evacuate the veterans on a train especially made up for that purpose, which had actually passed through the keys on one occasion, Sheldon waited until nearly noon, Monday, Labor Day, with the hurricane imminent, before phoning Ghent to order a train. Because Ghent was not available for nearly two hours, however, the train could not actually be ordered until around 2:00 P.M. As Loftin described it:

On September 2nd, which was Labor Day and a holiday, all General Offices of the Railway being closed, at 2:00 P.M. Mr. Ghent called [the] Assistant to the General Superintendent, at his home in St. Augustine, and requested a special train to go to the Veterans' Camps in the Keys, to take the men and their baggage and belongings from the camps to Hollywood, 18 miles north of Miami. At that time, owing to summer service being in operation, we had no switch engineer in service in Miami.

The assistant superintendent immediately gave instructions to proceed with the dispatching of the special train. However, the train had to be assembled one car at a time, and the engine had to be prepared and steamed up for the trip. The latter process, Loftin said, "under best conditions, takes two hours." The train was unable to leave until 4:25 P.M., nearly two and a half hours from the time of Ghent's call.[12]

Statements were obtained by investigators from everyone at the FEC involved in the dispatch of the rescue train, and all of the statements agreed on the timing and the circumstances involved. The most comprehensive was that of A. I. Pooser, FEC superintendent, who wrote:

After having advice August 31st and September 1st as to the probability of a hurricane passing near the south end of Florida, I decided that inasmuch as my Chief Clerk and other employees in the office may take the afternoon of Labor Day away from the office, that I would not even take the dinner hour away from the building. I had lunch in the restaurant downstairs under my office at about 1:30 P.M. When I walked upstairs, and entered the hall, which was some time between 1:45 P.M. and 2:10 P.M. . . . I was handed the 1:30 P.M. advisory report and advised by the train dispatcher that District Superintendent Gaddis wanted to talk to me on the railroad 'phone with reference to the probability of operating a relief train for the veterans to take them off of the keys. I answered the 'phone immediately and when I was advised by District Superintendent Gaddis that Mr. Sheldon, Assistant Director at Matecumbe, had telephoned his office that he (Sheldon) was asking the Jacksonville office for this relief train and in all probability we would get an order for it. I inquired to know where they were going and if they had made arrangements with the community in which we would take them, having in mind sanitary care, etc. The response from Mr. Gaddis was that he failed to make inquiry and Mr. Sheldon did not state. I immediately called the Chief Train Dispatcher and instructed to have Miami terminal begin gathering equipment for this train and see how many baggage cars and coaches they could get. I then called the telegraph operator at St. Augustine general office and requested him to telephone Mr. Aitcheson and say to him that if he was not going to return to the office please call me long distance on commercial line telephone; that I wanted to confer with him about a special train that would probably be ordered. I had in mind that if the Jacksonville Veterans' Office should order a train they would probably have difficulty in locating someone in the General Office building and I desired to extend to Mr. Aitcheson the advice we had as to the probability of a train being ordered. Mr. Aitcheson replied that he was on his way to the office and would call me in a few minutes. This was after 2:00 P.M. About 2:15 or perhaps a minute or so later, Mr. Aitcheson called me on railway telephone and stated he already had the order from the Jacksonville office for the train. We discussed the matter several minutes as to equipment, where they were going, and other details. I then called the Chief Train Dispatcher . . . and instructed him to contact Miami terminal forces and advise them to get the train started immediately, as we had the order for it, which was probably something like 2:35 P.M. . . . In a few minutes Chief Train Dispatcher came into my office and discussed with me the matter of what equipment we should give them and mentioned the fact that the Miami terminal forces had made some statement with reference to having to gather the equipment from different parts of the yard; for instance, the baggage cars at the express platform, one of the coaches was on the repair track, the other coaches were probably in two different places in the yard, excepting one that was on No. 33 as an extra coach and it would have to be switched from 33's train after the other equipment was assembled. I told the Chief Train Dispatcher I appreciated the various locations that the equipment may be in but to tell the terminal force to get out the train as quick as they could; anyhow not later than 4:00 P.M. Up until this time we had no idea that there was a near approach of the hurricane. However, if we should have had such information it probably would not have expedited the movement as the forces had dropped all other work and were concentrating on getting this train out.

When Pooser called at 4:00 P.M. to check on the train he was told that it would be about another fifteen minutes before it departed.

One reason was that we had supplied three FEC Railway ventilated box cars for equipment [on Nos. 75 and 76] in case the Veterans needed it and it would be necessary to change the air brake trips on the passenger equipment [on] account [of] handling freight cars. He also inquired to know if it would be satisfactory to head down to Lower Matecumbe and back out. I told him I did not think so; that it would be dark coming out and he better back into the Camp and head out in order that he would have headlight facilities. I cautioned him to be safe but at the same time to operate as fast as safety would permit and try to get out of the Camp before dark, or, anyhow, be loaded by dark. The train finally left Miami at 4:25 P.M.[13]

It is difficult to avoid the impression that Sheldon and Ghent had picked the worst possible time to order the relief train—from the standpoint of both the holiday circumstances at the railroad and the now-imminent danger from the hurricane—after passing up two easy opportunities to evacuate the men on Sunday. Confident that by a simple phone call he could activate a quick rescue operation by the FEC, Sheldon found that even communication with his own chain of command required two hours that he had not anticipated in his calculations. With over two hours of preparation time added to the time required for a normal trip to the keys, it was apparent that the train could not arrive at the camps until at least 8:00 P.M. It should have been equally obvious, however, that this would not be a normal trip. By waiting until too late to order the train, Sheldon had ensured that it would not be able to travel under normal weather conditions to the camps. In fact, Ghent himself calculated that the trip would probably take about eight hours, which was actually more time than the relief train took to reach the keys.[14] Ghent should have listened to Cutler. Instead, he trusted in Sheldon's judgment and preparations, both of which turned out to be inadequate. Ghent, however, was culpable in other ways. By ordering the additional equipment for Nos. 75 and 76, which had been kept on the trains on Monday in case it was needed, and then failing to make use of it, he needlessly complicated the task of assembling a relief train from the equipment available to the FEC on Monday.

Scott Loftin described the trip:

It was delayed 10 minutes at the Miami River drawbridge by a stream of holiday motor boats passing through the draw. As there are no means of turning an engine [around] south of Homestead the engine was turned at that point, and the train was backed from there towards the Veterans Camps. South of Homestead the train ran into gales, which continued to grow heavier, and the train reached Quarry, on Quarry Key, 72 miles south of Miami, at 6:50 P.M. There the train was delayed one hour and 20 minutes by obstruction resulting from the storm. When this was cleared up the train proceeded to Islamorada, where it arrived about 8:20 P.M. , where it was found that the wires were down, the agent had evacuated the station, the storm had become of hurricane force, and the water had risen to about the level of the floors of coaches. Finally a tidal wave came and turned over all the coaches, baggage cars, and the three freight cars, leaving only the engine standing on the track.

Loftin concluded that the veterans could have been evacuated safely only if the train had "left Miami about 10:00 A.M."[15]

William Johns, a *Miami Daily News* reporter, accompanied the train and wrote his own account of the trip:

I boarded the train at 7 P.M. Monday at Homestead. Over protest of the train crew, a half-dozen veterans anxious to return to their key camp and save their possessions joined the train there. We proceeded south, making the first stop, of necessity, opposite a rock quarry near Veterans Camp No. 1. A steel cable attached to a quarry crane caught one of the box cars and threatened to derail the train.

After a costly wait of almost an hour and a half while the train was freed of its obstruction we started south again, first picking up the superintendent of the stone quarry, his wife and child.

A handful of veterans who had sought refuge in the quarry also boarded the train.

In my opinion it would have been impossible to entrain the men from camp No. 1 when we came opposite for a brief stop. The wind was too high for a man to walk. Apparently the train crew decided to proceed under instruction to the two lower camps, if possible, and evacuate the men at camp No. 1 on the return.

There was no return. That train will never make another run.

As we neared Islamorada, the wind and water increased. The cars swayed on the rails. Most of the 25 persons aboard were in the two rear coaches. The water was slowing us to a snail's pace. It was dark and we expected momentarily the roadbed would give way.

Suddenly, just south of Islamorada, the water forced a stop. It was then well over the rail bed. We had been stopped by 10 or 15 minutes when a wall of water from 15 to 20 feet high picked up our coaches and swirled them about like straws.

We felt them going and I imagine everyone thought it was the end. I know I did.

We came out of the swirl of water with a thump that tossed the inmates of the coaches across seats, against windows, and in crazy heaps on sidewalls that had suddenly become floors. Miraculously, none was hurt severely.

The wall of water passed as quickly as it came, else we would all have been drowned like rats in a trap.

It was daylight before we could determine exactly what had happened. Meanwhile, the wind, which I am certain was more than 100 miles an hour during the worst of the storm before midnight, hammered at our overturned coaches.

It was a terrifying night. Our greatest worry was that another tidal wave would come. The wind seemed tame in comparison to the fear of drowning. But outside the shelter the wind was a killer.

Morning came and we surveyed our escape with wonderment. The last car and the next to it in which most of us were riding had been carried 100 feet and 40 feet, respectively, from the tracks. Up toward the head of the train the seven other coaches spread fanwise to the left of the right of way on which the engine only and its tender remained.

One of the box cars on the rear of the 11-car train had been carried 150 feet from the roadbed.

We stayed in another box car nearer the right of way until winds permitted walking. Then we started back on foot. It took me a day, a night and half of another day to reach Homestead, only about 30 miles away. Not much is left of the highway. The water has sheared great slices off the keys.

I know nothing of what might have happened south of where our train was swept from its tracks. But the keys to the southward are even more exposed than is the place where the tidal wave struck us.

"That same wave must have swept Lower Matecumbe," he wrote. "I don't see how any living thing, exposed to that rush of water, could have survived."[16]

When asked later by investigators whether he thought the veterans could have been evacuated, he replied:

A. Yes, sir! Absolutely! From what I have heard—

Q. I thought you said you didn't imagine this blow was coming till Tuesday?

A. I didn't! But why leave those men down there? Here's the question I can't solve, for myself. Those poor devils—of course, it was right after pay day, and a lot of them were drunk; a lot of them they would have had to carry to the train; and a lot wouldn't have got on, of course, and that's all true; but the thing I can't figure out for the life of me is that when they first began to get those storm warnings, and they had any idea it would come there at all, with that number of men, and the temperament of those men, and there are men, cases of "psycho" as they call it, and knowing the wild way that those men would run around, why, early Monday morning they weren't taken out and brought either to Homestead or Miami until the storm period had passed.[17]

Camp director Ray Sheldon, who boarded the train at Islamorada, described his experience:

At 5:30, those remaining at the Office in Matecumbe went to Islamorada, where we were told that the train had just left Homestead. The wind was then blowing about 50 to 60 miles an hour, not sufficient to cause me any effort in standing outside. In a very short time it had increased enough to cause us to leave the station office and go to a box car. About 8:15 P.M. I noticed a flashing of a light, and I left the box car and had to struggle against a headwind for about fifty (50) feet, in order to reach the relief train.

When I left the box car, the ground was dry and traveling this fifty (50) feet, the water raised to my waist. Getting into the cab of the engine, I instructed the engineer to start the train to Camp No. 3.

The engineer informed me that the wind had blown the train down that far, without the use of steam. In looking out of the cab, the water was going so fast by the step of the cab, that I thought we were going at a dangerous speed, and ordered the engineer to slow up. In attempting to put on the brakes, he found the air-brakes had locked. The engineer thought he had lost a car and a broken air-line had caused the brakes to set.

Mr. Perdue immediately left the locomotive cab to disconnect this car. When Perdue left the cab, the water was half way between his waist and arm pits. At that time the water was so high, it extinguished the fire in the engine. It was then 8:20 P.M.

Upon inquiring from the engineer and fireman what time they had left Miami, I was told they were asked to report at 4:00 P.M., and had not left Miami until 4:25 P.M. I understand from the engine crew they stopped at Homestead and picked up a Section gang and Section motor power hand car and its crew, and swapped their engine end to end.

As the train passed by the quarry where we were removing rock for the bridge, a guy line from the Stiff Log Derrick had fallen across the track and had hooked onto the locomotive cab, and caused a delay of one hour to remove the wire.

The water had risen so, that from the light available, it appeared to be on a level with the cab floor; and from 8:20 P.M. on, the engine could not be moved. The waves were of such height that they beat over the heads of the engine crew who were in the cab of the locomotive. We remained in this position until dawn of Tuesday morning, when we found that the cars of this train had been bodily lifted from the track and set to the West a distance of fifty (50) to seventy-five (75) feet. The engine was the only part of the train remaining on its track. . . .

We found whole colonies of houses were swept in to one point by the current of water; sometimes causing a pile of debris to the height of 20 to 25 feet. Land marks and houses which were pointed to with pride by the natives as being storm resisting, were swept from their foundations. From Snake Creek to as far South as Carribee, there are only two buildings remaining; namely, the lower floor of the Matecumbe Hotel and a Filling Station owned by Mr. O. D. King, who turned his place into a first aid hospital.[18]

In the months before the hurricane, concerned veterans had been assured by the camp directors that they would be evacuated well in advance of any danger. One veteran recalled that he had asked Ghent in April "what provision had been made for the men on the Keys in the event that a hurricane warning came in." Ghent had replied "that he had already made arrangements with the F.E.C. Railroad to have two trains with cooking equipment in the baggage cars, to take care of the men, and that the men would be hauled from the Keys at the first warning."[19] Another, from a different camp, recalled that in May, Ghent had told them that "he had made arrangements with the Florida East Coast Railway Company to get us out within five hours in case of a storm and that they knew at least five (5) days before a storm, that he had three barometers and he had a man stationed at the barometers to watch them and he had three so that if one went wrong he would have the other two to depend on."[20] A veteran from Camp 3 told investigators that when Ghent first took over the camps he told the veterans that he had made arrangements for a train to be ordered "48 hours before a storm came to get us out." On the day of the hurricane, "the men had confidence in that and thought the train would get there."[21]

To reconstruct the events in the camp leading up to the ordering of the train, it must be recalled that both Sheldon and Ghent were away from the camp—the former in Key West, the latter in Jacksonville. According to Sheldon's secretary, he had designated no one to be in charge during his absence despite the presence of a storm in the Caribbean. Shortly after Sheldon left, however, Sam Cutler, works director, arrived at camp headquarters and took charge. As weather reports grew more threatening, Cutler, in the words of Sheldon's secretary, "was very much excited and we couldn't get Mr. Sheldon on the phone." Cutler then phoned Ghent in Jacksonville and told him: "If you will give me authority, I will take charge of the situation." But Ghent told Cutler that Sheldon would handle the situation. Although some at headquarters thought that Cutler was unduly alarmed, Cutler apparently based his concern on what he had been told by old-timers with hurricane experience who thought that the situation looked bad. Cutler had also called the FEC before he talked to Ghent, to see how long it would take for a train to arrive at the camps.[22] A little later Sunday morning, Sheldon arrived by ferry from Key West.

According to the testimony of John Good, general storekeeper of the camps, who overheard the telephone conversation between Cutler and Ghent, Cutler told the latter "that from all indications we were going to have some very nasty weather, that the barometer was falling every few minutes, and that from what information he could gather barometer readings were considerably higher in Key West and Miami than they were on the Keys, leading him to believe that we would shorty have an exceptionally high wind." Cutler wanted to move the veterans out, but Ghent refused to take any action until Sheldon was on the scene. Asked whether Cutler had relayed this opinion to Sheldon once the latter had arrived at headquarters from Key West, Good remarked that he had, as had others, but that "Mr. Sheldon was rather hard to advise on that or any other subject," and had been from the time he had first assumed the duties of director of the camps. Cutler, he concluded, would "have avoided an extremely bad situation and saved many lives had he been in authority Sunday and Monday."[23] Frederick Poock, sixty-two-year-old office manager and trust officer for the camps, agreed, testifying:

This is just an opinion, but I think that had Cutler been given authority to act, the train would have been called in time to evacuate the men to points of safety. I feel that Mr. Ghent's attitude to Mr. Cutler at the time he made his request for authority was reprehensible, in view of the fact that he was some hundreds of miles away from the scene and Mr. Cutler was right there pleading for authority to act.[24]

At 11:46 A.M. Sheldon placed a call for Ghent in Jacksonville, apparently intending to get his authorization to order the train, but was unable to reach him.[25] Ghent returned the call nearly two hours later, at 1:37 P.M. When asked why Sheldon was unable to reach him any earlier, Ghent replied that he had left his hotel between 11:00 and 11:30 A.M. and had gone directly to his office, whereupon he had left for lunch and "returned to the office between 1:00 and 1:30 at which time I was informed that the long distance operator at Miami was trying to get in touch with me." Ghent had not left word with the hotel operator where he could be found, nor had he left word with the long-distance operator.[26] Asked how much time he thought was available to evacuate the veterans from the time he ordered the train at around 2:00 P.M. on Monday, Ghent replied that he "thought we had from ten to fifteen hours in which to operate before the storm could possibly reach the Keys." Ghent had reached this conclusion by "locating the storm two hundred miles east of Havana and approximately a hundred and fifty miles southeast of Matecumbe Key and the storm moving at its estimated rate of speed of eight miles an hour."[27] Even if Ghent's calculations had been correct, this was cutting the margin to a good deal less than the forty-eight hours he had promised the veterans. Still, had Ghent not been inaccessible by telephone during those critical two hours, or had Sheldon called earlier when Cutler, at least, thought was appropriate, an additional two hours might have made it possible for the train to succeed in its rescue mission.

William A. Hardaker, superintendent of the works program at Camp 1, testified that he would have ordered the train on Sunday morning. Hardaker was asked by investigators: "If the railroad company had notified the FERA by correspondence and former conferences that it would require five hours to get a train down there and three hours' notice to get the train ready and that was known to the officials [in charge of the camps], you think there was carelessness and negligence in ordering the train?" He answered: "Absolutely; yes, sir—8 hours; that would make 8 hours? Yessiree and if I had known there was that much time required I would have marched my men out."[28]

E. H. Sheeran, superintendent of construction, told investigators that he had not put much faith in weather reports that located the hurricane two hundred miles away. He had said "To Hell with what they say; our barometer shows we are in a low area." He added: "I didn't pay much attention to the weather bureau when the barometer went down so fast, because for years I was down on the keys, and I studied those things, and we didn't have any weather bureau to give us that information."[29] So certain was

Sheeran that the hurricane was imminent that he not only secured the equipment for the Overseas Bridge Project, but also warned his civilian secretary to leave on Sunday night. His secretary recalled:

I was relieving Mr. Kelly on the barometer reading and telephones at such time as he was not there, running messages from such barometer and telephone to Col. Sheeran. This was on Sunday. At about noon Col. Sheeran, not having any control over the veterans, told those in authority that it looked pretty bad and that these men should be gotten out of camp, otherwise there would be a terrible loss of life because the majority of the men had had no experience in combating hurricanes. These two parties were Messrs. Cutler and Patterson of veterans headquarters staff, they being civilians. These two gentlemen stated that Mr. Sheldon, the man in charge of headquarters was in Key West and would return on the ferry. When the ferry arrived I neither saw Mr. Sheldon nor have I seen him to this day. On Sunday night Col. Sheeran suggested that I go to Miami or Homestead to get out of the storm and be safe. I told him I did not feel like going and leaving him and some other men in the office. I therefore remained in camp. The next morning, still being a holiday, the men were somewhat excited and there were all sorts of rumors that the train was enroute.[30]

The headquarters of the camps during this crucial period was a scene of concern on the part of some that was in sharp contrast with the apparent serenity of Sheldon, who consulted the maps and barometers and played cards with some of the staff. Robert Ayer, Jr., assistant communications clerk under Sheldon, recalled that "one of the locals, Mr. Parker, . . . kept coming into the office on Sunday to tell them that there was going to be a big storm. Nobody took him very seriously, except Cutler, who was the most nervous of the people at headquarters." Ayer reported receiving a message from the weather bureau at 2:00 A.M. on Monday warning their location of "high tides and strong gales." Ayer notified Pattison and went back to sleep, then repeated the information to Sheldon after he got up at 7:30 A.M. Not until shortly after 11:00 A.M., however, did Sheldon decide to order the train, at which point he called Hollywood to make arrangements for the reception of the veterans and tried to call Ghent. At one point his questioner asked him: "You people were just sitting around waiting for the danger to become immediate, were you?" Asked if there were anything he would like to add to his statement, Ayer said he believed the train should have been at the camps by Sunday; he did not "believe in waiting until the last minute for anything."[31]

Captain J. T. Wiggington, clothing supply officer at the camps, testified that Parker had also come to his house at 8:00 A.M. on Monday morning and asked to borrow a hammer. He told Wigginton: "My barometer is falling, and I am going to board up my house," and "Captain, I don't know about that weather bureau in Miami. They say there is no danger, but my barometer is falling, and I am not going to take any chance." Wiggington found that when he went to work he "couldn't keep my back door open, and it was too dark to work in there, and I gathered my work up and took it up to Mr. Sheldon's office, and then I began to get nervous." They began to play cards, "anything to pass the time; we were all just waiting on those damn weather reports."[32]

Conrad Van Hyning, Florida ERA administrator, was trying on Monday morning to get a telephone call through to Sheldon at the camp headquarters, but failed to reach him. He finally called M. E. Gilfond, the FERA administrator for Key West and asked him to try to get through. Van Hyning's concern was apparently shared by the FERA in Washington. He recalled for investigators:

On Monday morning when the newspapers carried the story that the storm was proceeding in the same general direction I tried to get Mr. Sheldon at the camp on the telephone and while I was trying to get Mr. Sheldon, Mr. Perry Fellows, Chief Engineer of the FERA and the WPA telephoned me from Washington around 10:00 in the morning and his conversation was generally that he wanted to know what provision we had made to evacuate the veterans; that he had lost friends on the bridge when it was built and was concerned. . . . He told me he had just talked with Mr. Aubrey Williams, Assistant Administrator, FERA, and that they both felt that proper precautions should be taken and that they were checking to be sure the veterans were gotten out on time. I was unable to get Mr. Sheldon on the telephone direct—I learned the reason was that the phone was busy. I did get Mr. Gilfond, FERA Administrator in Key West. I got him around 11 o'clock and asked him what he knew of the situation and asked whether he had talked to Mr. Sheldon. He said he talked to Mr. Sheldon, and Mr. Sheldon said they could have the train brought down within 3 hours after they had given notice. I asked him to get in touch with Mr. Sheldon again and get me further information as to what they were doing. Then in about another hour my call to Gilfond or his report back to me somewhere around 12 or 1 o'clock came through and at that time I told Mr. Gilfond to have Mr. Sheldon bring the train to Islamorada and have it stand by on the Keys rather than to take a chance on the 3-hour wait. That was the only definite instructions I gave to bring the train down immediately and not wait for the 3 hours notice. That was about 1 o'clock.[33]

Gilfond testified:

that Mr. Van Hyning called him at Key West, Fla. before noon on September 2, 1935, and stated that he had been trying to get in touch with Mr. Ray Sheldon at the Veterans' camps but that he had been unable to do so; that Mr. Van Hyning requested that he, Mr. Gilfond, get in touch with Sheldon and tell him he was concerned about the Veterans in the camps on the Keys and did not want him to take any chances whatever. Mr. Gilfond stated that he immediately telephoned Mr. Sheldon and gave him Mr. Van Hyning's message and that in reply Mr. Sheldon stated that he had the matter well in hand, that he had commandeered a train and could have it ordered out on a moment's notice; also that he (Sheldon) could not understand why Mr. Van Hyning could not reach him by phone.[34]

Asked if he thought there had been any dereliction of duty, Van Hyning said:

No, I can't say that, but I do have this one feeling that perhaps I should have anticipated and perhaps others should have antici- pated—a possible situation which would not conform to what was reported, that perhaps to be on the completely safe side we should have pulled those boys out in the morning. I didn't feel that until afterwards. At the time it seemed that everybody knew what was going on.[35]

In later testimony, Van Hyning added:

If Mr. Sheldon did not have information that the train was ready or could be made ready in a few minutes I would say he was negligent. I would say he was negligent if he didn't check the facts sufficiently so that there would be a safe margin to get the men out; if he had allowed the train to be unchecked for a period of 10 hours before they expected the storm to hit, but if he had checked it, had felt safe about it and felt they had a period of time to get out, then he couldn't be considered negligent.[36]

A memorandum of a conversation between an investiga- tor and Sam Cutler is revealing of the inhibitions the men faced in testifying:

During the course of the discussion, Mr. Cutler . . . voluntarily stated that up until approximately six months ago Mr. Ghent was a very fine man, agreeable to get along with, but that subsequent to that time, apparently his job had gone to his head and that he had trusted no one except his immediate assistants. This volun- tary statement was made notwithstanding previous reiterations

that he and Mr. Ghent had always been friendly and that he had
a very high personal regard for Mr. Ghent. And further on in the
discussion he asked Mr. Kennamer for his opinion of his testimony and Mr. Kennamer replied substantially that it was good
but that he felt that [Cutler] had been a little too lenient with
those in authority over him, to which he replied by asking: "Do
you blame me?"[37]

PREPARATIONS ALL AROUND THEM

Other "locals" were also taking precautions. The owner
of the Matecumbe Hotel, which had been leased to the
FERA as their headquarters, did not think that the hurricane would hit the keys, but knew enough about the unpredictability of tropical storms to take precautions. By
Sunday night he and his father had managed to board up
the hotel, except for a few windows that they "could get
quick, if the wind came up."[38] R. W. Craig, owner of a
yacht supply business, a store, a camp, and a two-hundred-
foot service dock, spent all day Sunday preparing his buildings for a storm.[39] Another resident of the keys, who lived
about six hundred yards from the Lower Matecumbe
camp, testified that his barometer readings had made him
certain by Sunday that the storm would hit. He had, he
said, "everything under control" by about 4:00 P.M.
Sunday: "Everything battened down, fastened up; could
not do any more." He did not convey his concern to the
veterans' camp, but recalled that two weeks before the
hurricane he had given his opinion of the camp to one of
the officials from headquarters. He told the official that
"we had high tides in October, higher than any time of the
year. I said in October the tides will put that mess hall
under water." The veterans in the camp, he said, "didn't
have anything but tents. I saw them blown to pieces with a
common north wind. I saw a big tent for storing things

there one night and next morning it would be all to pieces." The men, he said, were living in tents, but "they were not allowed to say so," and there were some wooden buildings, but the latter were "only stuck up, not built." Asked whether he thought it was "safe to maintain a camp for veterans on the Keys during the months of September and October," he answered, "I do not."[40]

The postmaster at Islamorada testified that the veterans should not have been left in the camps later than Sunday. "The indications were there would be a storm. When there is a storm in the straits we always get a heavy wind of it." He explained:

You see, their situation was different from ours. Those in Camp #1 were in a very low piece of land, right open to the sea. Any sea at all would sweep it. There was nothing to shelter them in their little huts at all. No anchorage—they were just set upon piers and I told them some time ago when they first built them that they had better tie them down or if we had a storm they wouldn't have the huts when the storm was over.

The veterans, he concluded, should not have been on the keys in temporary buildings during the hurricane season.[41]

Albert Buck, general foreman of Camp 5, lived with a "local" who had a barometer. The barometer began to drop on Saturday and continued to drop on Sunday. He went to headquarters at 11:00 A.M. on Sunday to find Cutler still in charge. Cutler tried to get authority to order a train, but failed. On Monday morning the barometer was still dropping, but he thought that the train must by now be on its way. The superintendent of his camp came back from headquarters "around 11 or 12 o'clock" and told him that nothing had been done about the train, that "the men were sitting in headquarters and . . . didn't seem to know that the wind was blowing outside. He said it was perfectly calm up at headquarters and they hadn't come out to look things over, and they hadn't ordered a train at that time." Not until about 1:00 P.M. did Cutler inform them that the train had finally been ordered. Buck concluded that the directors of the camp had "waited too long. In other words, on Sunday Mr. Sheldon was in Key West honeymooning; Mr. Ghent was in Jacksonville or some other place; and we were getting reports . . . from all over the country that this storm was approaching, and Mr. Cutler was here in charge without any authority." He told the investigators:

[I]t was the consensus of opinion by all the men including myself that in case of a storm that we would all be taken care of in plenty of time, taken out of there in plenty of time, so the storm wouldn't slip up on us and injure us, and we would be looked out for; so consequently the camps never made any provision for a storm, because we figured it would be done from the higher authorities.[42]

Fred Bonner, Jr., watchman at Camp 1, told investigators that he had not been apprehensive of the arrival of a hurricane, because he was not familiar with them. He and many of the other men were certain that the hurricane would hit, because they had been told so by a local fisherman. They never received any word from headquarters about it but heard Sunday morning that hurricane warnings had been posted, and they were interested in seeing what one was like. "We all hoped it would blow the mosquitoes away and cool things off; that's as much as they thought of it; that is, the majority." As for the reasons why the veterans were not removed in time, Bonner told the investigators: "I believe it was the customary unconcern that Mr. F. B. Ghent showed towards the veterans and their welfare."[43]

According to D. A. Malcolm, auditor at the camps, Sheldon held a meeting with John Good, Sam Cutler, and him on Sunday. The majority of them thought the train should be ordered so that the men could be gotten out. Sheldon, however, gave them "to understand that he was in charge and would take care of the situation." Malcolm's opinion was that the train should have been ordered to Islamorada and held there, not in Miami, in case it was needed. He blamed Sheldon for the delay in ordering the train.[44]

F. L. Meyers, in charge of the fresh water supply for Camp 3, recalled that Colonel Sheeran, superintendent of construction on the bridge project, had told somebody from headquarters on Sunday afternoon that all indications pointed to a terrific storm, and, in Meyers's words, "that it would be suicide not to move the men out of the camp, and that some steps should be taken at once to provide transportation, either by train or by use of our own motor transportation, to evacuate at once." These, he recalled, "were his exact words." Sheeran told him on Monday that he had "several times reported this warning to those who had authority." Meyers later talked to Paul Pugh, general foreman at Camp 3, who told him he had telephoned Sheldon"and had even gone so far as to tell Mr. Sheldon that if transportation were not provided, or assurances of transportation given at once, that the men would leave of their own accord; and that Mr. Sheldon informed him that if we attempted to leave the camp, that we would be stopped by the Florida National Guard."[45]

Eugene A. Pattison, field engineer at the camps under Sheldon, revealed another possible reason for the delay. After the investigator had described the Sheldon and Ghent telephone calls on Monday, he added: "Then one hour and fifty-one minutes was lost in getting Mr. Ghent to order the train. That delay was because Mr. Ghent did not keep himself available." Pattison responded: "That is what it was. When we got in touch with Miami, after we had spoken about the train, they wanted to know who would pay for it. Then we had to get in touch with Jacksonville and St. Augustine." Pattison was under the impression, from the FEC station agent at Islamorada, that a train was

waiting at Miami to be dispatched "at a moment's notice."
This, however, would have been the train arriving from
Key West, which was, in fact, ready to leave if called. But it
was not called. Pattison wrongly inferred that the train had
been ordered by his superiors to stand ready to leave
whenever it was needed. It had not been. Aware that the
FEC had notified the camps in writing that they required
twelve hours notice, Pattison agreed that the failure of
the camp officials to order the railroad amounted to
negligence.[46]

Sheldon was apparently under the impression that a
train could be dispatched from Miami and take them out of
the keys on three hours notice. One of the veterans overheard Sheldon's conversations with Ghent on Sunday afternoon. At that time Ghent informed Sheldon that, in the
veteran's words, "he had already made arrangements for
trains at Miami, that these trains were standing ready at
Miami and could be taken down on a three-hour notice,
take us out of there on a three-hour notice." Sheldon then
made the phone call to Gaddis to confirm Ghent's statement, and Gaddis told him of the train just arrived from
Key West, which could be dispatched immediately if
needed. This seemed to verify what Ghent had said, but of
course it did not. The time discussed applied, in fact, only
to the train already steamed up and ready to depart, not to
a train that might later have to be put together on a
holiday. Sheldon then called Ghent back and discussed the
matter with him again, telling him, in part, that the veterans were not yet very excited about the hurricane. The
state of mind of the veterans, of course, hardly should have
been a factor in preparations.[47]

William M. Johns, a reporter for the *Miami Daily News*,
recalled that he had heard rumors that, "there was a
squabble between the Florida East Coast Railroad and the
Administration in Washington as to who was going to pay
for it; and I know it is a lot of bunk, so there is no use

taking up your time with it."[48] One veteran, however, testified that members of the train crew had told a number of veterans that the train had been delayed over the question of payment of $300 for it.[49] There is no evidence that this was the case.

Not everybody was as unprepared as the veterans' camps. In addition to the example of the "locals," busily boarding up and otherwise securing their possessions, the ferry from Key West was tied up on Sunday, following its arrival, to weather the storm. This action made an impression on many of the veterans. One told investigators: "You take that ferry down there. Why did they take precautions and tie up that ferry the way they did? It was scheduled to go back—it came in about noon and pulled back about one. It didn't go out on the following day. The ferry is still there. It is these things that make a person stop and wonder why it was the other authorities didn't take a little more precautions."[50] Another was asked if the veterans were worried about the storm as early as Sunday. He answered: "Yes, they were. I tell you the reason. That ferry boat came in Sunday and they tied her up and would not leave her return. Another thing, bunch of sponge pickers, this one fellow that was head of it, said they ordered him into land; a hurricane on the road and they came this way and tied up."[51] For yet another, the tying up of the ferry boat was evidence that "they knew the storm was coming. They tied up the ferry boat on Friday [sic] and we were tied up on the keys."[52] Another veteran recalled: "When I seen the ferry tied up, I thought it was something wrong; then I couldn't understand why they didn't get us men out of there."[53] Another observed: "I can't understand why we were not evacuated since they had pulled in all the floating machinery on Saturday afternoon and had tied the ferry boat. . . . I cannot understand why machinery was taken care of and human lives left endangered."[54]

The equipment used in the Overseas Bridge Project was also secured against the hurricane well before it hit. A

veteran from Camp 3 recalled that at 5:30 A.M. Sunday
morning "they called in the fellows that had been manning
all the machinery, running the boats and things like that; at
5:30 in the morning, they started taking all the machinery
off the water in a channel that they had been a month and
a half digging, to store the machinery."[55] Another testified:
"All floating equipment used in building the bridge, such
as dredges, sand suckers, pile drivers, etc. were taken into
a narrow channel in the back of the island, that had been
provided for that purpose."[56] William Knox also reported
that "on Sunday morning when we got out of bed they
were moving all of the machinery to the hurricane channel
that they had dug to put that machinery in."[57] B. M. Duncan, consulting engineer for the State Road Department on
the bridge project, recalled that it was impossible to know
where the storm would hit. He added:

That was a mean storm to track for this reason. It originated back
in the islands where there is very little transportation. . . . The
best we could have were barometer readings. We didn't know
where the storm was going. We knew that it was likely to turn
and go anywhere at any time. We were uneasy and put all our
equipment in Hurricane Creek. We moved our equipment in
there on Sunday and continued to make fast and tie up all through
Monday as long as we could work. But we have tied up equipment before and a great many times the storm didn't hit. It gets to
be a habit but we know the danger well enough to take all precautions. If it doesn't hit you may feel like a monkey, but if it does hit,
you feel that you have taken the precautions that were necessary.

Duncan pointed out that "a newcomer would not have as
much fear of these storms as one who has been through
them. It is possible that they would not know all the precautions that Sheeran would know."[58]

E. H. Sheeran, superintendent of construction at the
camps, testified that he had begun to secure the equipment
at about 6:00 A.M., Sunday.

I had a hurricane harbor dug out about 17 or 1800 feet long, up in the woods, and six o'clock that night I had it all put away, and tied up; and after that I had to pick up the men off the keys, on account of it being a holiday, or Sunday, and get it all tied up, and during the day, anybody that wanted to leave, I sent them out of there, because the barometer kept dropping all the time.

Q. Sunday?

A. Yes, sir; and they got kind of scary; so Monday it commenced to get pretty bad, and some of the boys had come down from Miami and I drove them all back; I sent all back that I could spare, and the rest were down to stay with me; I was going to stay, and so they stayed.

Q. You mean the civilian employees?

A. Yes, sir.[59]

It was Sheeran's concern about the approaching storm, and his actions to protect the equipment, that apparently motivated Sam Cutler to make equivalent provision for the veterans in the camps by ordering a train on Sunday.[60] Sheeran repeatedly pressed on Sheldon the necessity to order a train, but without results until the phone call to Ghent on Monday.

DRUNKS AND TRUCKS

One issue that clouded the rescue question was the condition of the veterans that weekend. Had the veterans in the camps been so intoxicated that it would have been difficult and time-consuming to round them up and load them on the train, even if it had arrived with some time to spare? The general storekeeper of the camps testified that there had been a good deal of drinking at the time of the hurricane. He told investigators:

Friday was payday in the camps and Monday being Labor Day was a holiday; there had always been considerable drunkenness in these camps on paydays, but with the additional holiday and also with the mental strain caused the veterans by the repeated newspaper articles and statements reported to have come from Mr. Hopkins' office [FERA in Washington] that the veterans' camps would be done with in a very short while these men who didn't leave the camp for the holidays were drinking more heavily than I had seen them over a period of about a year since the camp began. I might say that a minimum of 75 percent of the men in the camps were drinking a few hours before the hurricane and that 50 percent of those drinking were in a drunken condition. I believe that I am in a position to make this statement without fear of contradiction, having been in every camp several times and just previous to the hurricane.

Asked who controlled the source of supply, the store-keeper replied that beer could be obtained from canteens in the camps as well from "various sources in the community." Bootleggers supplying hard liquor were nearly impossible to keep out of the chain of small islands.[61]

Others agreed that, as one veteran put it, "about seventy-five per cent of them were under the influence of whiskey and beer" and "didn't have sense enough to realize what [the hurricane] was all about."[62] Others, however, disagreed. Thomas Harrell testified that "every man was in condition where he could have saved himself; I don't think there was any of the men down where they couldn't have taken care of themselves."[63]

In the absence of Ray Sheldon, Sam Cutler issued orders for the canteens of the three veterans' camps to stop selling beer late Monday morning. In retrospect this seems to have been a sensible move, for if the men were intoxicated it could only complicate efforts to get them and their belongings on a relief train. Upon his return to the camp from Key West, however, Sheldon countermanded Cutler's order, calling it "silly."[64] Yet, as the chief deputy sheriff of the camps pointed out, it took more time to handle a drunken man than a sober one, and the possibility that drunken men would have to be dealt with should have dictated that

the train be ordered even earlier than under other circumstances. The chief deputy sheriff himself estimated that 50
to 60 percent of the veterans were very intoxicated the
weekend of the hurricane. He also affirmed that there
were enough trucks to evacuate the veterans and that he
would have used them.[65]

The condition of the men has a bearing upon the possibility that the veterans might have been evacuated through
use of the motor transport available in the camps. When
questioned about this possibility, Fred Ghent replied it
would have been "impossible," because the camps "did
not have a sufficient number of trucks."[66] Ray Sheldon
likewise testified that there were only "six trucks in
constant use, and due to being used so much they were not
in first-class shape." Sheldon added that it "would not
have been safe, with the condition of a good many of the
men due to a pay day, to start them on a trip on an open
truck, any distance."[67] Of course, if Sheldon had, in fact,
ordered the canteens reopened on Monday, he had contributed to any such condition on the part of the men.

The preponderance of testimony by the veterans, themselves, however, contradicted the statements of Ghent and
Sheldon. Eugene A. Pattison, field engineer at the camps
under Sheldon, testified that the camps had "eight or ten
pickup trucks and about ten or twelve stake-body trucks,
also, dump trucks." Asked how many men could have
been taken out with this number of trucks, Pattison
replied, "All of them." Asked if he meant they could all
have been evacuated at the same time, Pattison affirmed
that he did. He added: "We have carried at least thirty-five
to a ball game in one truck and fifty could get in them."
Asked if anything had been said "at any time about using
the motor transportation," Pattison replied: "Not to my
knowledge."[68] The general foreman of Camp 5 testified
that his camp had "one stake-body truck and a pickup,
which could on an emergency have brought out from 50 to

60 men at one load," but nothing had been said about using them because "we thought we was being looked out for by the officials higher up, and when we saw that we was not, why it was too late to make any preparations."[69]

The recreational director of the veterans' camps testified that there was no question in his mind that the men could have evacuated by motor transportation. He told investigators:

We had plenty of gasoline, dump and stake body trucks at Camp #3 and at the Quarry at Snake Creek. They were all in good condition and I saw them at the Quarry when I got gasoline for my car between 12:00 and 1:00 P.M. to return back to Miami, Monday. So far as the men being in a drunken condition that they could not have been trusted to drive them out, there were several civilians connected with our office who were not drunk and could drive cars.[70]

Other Camp 1 veterans told investigators that there were plenty of men sober enough to take the trucks out and that there were enough trucks to take every man out.[71] A survivor of Camp 5 suggested that investigators look at "the *trucks* (so many of them) on the North side of Snake Creek—a mass of twisted wreckage, laying there among the remains of the storm. I contend, and can prove beyond doubt, we had trucks both of the ton or more type and lighter ones to move both men and their clothes."[72]

A veteran from Camp 3 likewise testified that "if the boys had keys to the trucks down there, there would have been more lives saved than there was; they should have loaded them on there and drove the hell out of there." He insisted that there were enough trucks and drivers.[73] Another Camp 3 veteran told investigators:

I would like to make this clear. I do not know whether it is newspaper talk or what. There were very few drunk and that was not holding them there. Everyone had all their things, including beds, ready to go. It seems as though, that is that had we been warned, we could have gotten out of there with trucks. There were trucks enough in our camp to take us all out.[74]

Yet another from Camp 3 insisted that all the men in his camp were sober.[75] A truck driver from Camp 3 affirmed that all of the men in all of the camps could have been evacuated in the trucks. Asked why he had not driven to safety, the truck driver reported that Sheeran had taken the keys from the box and had them in his pocket.[76]

Paul Pugh, top sergeant of Camp 3, told investigators:

There . . . was enough motor transportation at our camp to take every single man out of camp on trucks. To be exact there were three stake bodies that would hold forty men apiece, three dump trucks that would hold seventeen, and an ambulance that would hold at least sixteen. They were regularly in use around camp to go to ball games, shows, and what not.

He was also "very positive" that drivers were available for all of the trucks, and he had no idea why the motor transportation was not used. Pugh noted that Sheldon had been sufficiently concerned about his wife, at least, that he had gotten her off the keys well before the hurricane struck. Asked if he thought somebody had been "guilty of carelessness or negligence" in not getting the veterans out, Pugh answered: "Yes; put that down in big letters." He would, himself, have evacuated the men on Sunday afternoon, based on Sheeran's experience and concern.[77] Although Pugh did not mention it, one veteran testified that he had overheard Pugh beg Sheldon "to let the boys leave the camp in trucks, and Sheldon refused and stated that he was running the camp."[78]

In an interview with the *Miami Herald* from his hospital bed, Pugh said that he

began calling at Sheldon's house noon on Sunday when things looked like the blow was coming. I kept on going to Sheldon's house every few hours as the men were showing signs of unrest, but each time, Sheldon said there was no danger. . . . When I went to Sheldon's house on Sunday at about 9 o'clock, I was told there would be no danger for at least 48 hours, if there was to be any at all. I couldn't believe it because things just didn't look right to me or any of the other men. I went back again Monday at 10 A.M. and was told there was nothing to worry about and later in the day C. G. Sain, a civilian timekeeper, said there was going to be a train at 5:30.[79]

When several veterans went to Pugh on Monday afternoon to get permission to leave by truck, Pugh told them "that the rescue train would be after us and that the keys to the trucks had been collected."[80]

The civilian timekeeper at Camp 3 testified that his camp had only one pickup truck and one stake-body truck, but also the trucks that belonged to the Overseas Bridge Project which were under Colonel Sheeran's control. When asked how many trips would have been required with the two trucks of the camp in order to remove the veterans from Camp 3 to the Florida mainland, he replied that three would have been required to take them to Homestead and that it would have taken some time because there were governors on the trucks that restricted them to a top speed of 35 to 40 mph. If they had started Monday morning they could have made it, he concluded, but not if they had waited until Monday afternoon, at least not "without piling on like cordwood."[81] Sheeran, himself, testified that he had "quite a few trucks down there. I don't know just how many—about four dump trucks and three stake-bodies where I was." But after about 2:00 P.M. he considered that the "road was too slippery and it was too squally and there was nothing to protect them and water was over the roads." He was asked:

Q. You would not have attempted to use this transportation when the train didn't arrive?

A. That would have been impossible.

Q. I mean, if you knew the train was not going to arrive in time would you have moved the men by motor transportation?

A. There was nobody to say that the train was not going to arrive in time. It was a matter of using judgment. . . .

Q. Do you know if one reason the motor transportation was not used was because the men were not in condition to drive?

A. They were not in condition. They had been drinking.[82]

Thus, the condition of the veterans aside, the man who held the keys to the trucks that would have been needed to evacuate the veterans by that method was convinced that road conditions had rendered that option impossible by 2:00 P.M.

But if an evacuation by truck was possible on Monday morning, why was its use not considered, especially when Sheldon was unable for two critical hours to get through to Ghent for authorization to order the train? One Camp 1 veteran recalled that late Monday morning he and his foreman, O. D. King, had taken a ton-and-a-half pickup truck and used it to haul "the women from Matecumbe to the hospital at Camp No. 1." At this time, King told him that he had the keys to all trucks and had orders not to release them.[83] King was superintendent of transportation at the camps. If anyone had known what motor transportation was available, it would presumably have been the superintendent of transportation. Asked what vehicles he had, and their capacity, King testified that there were in the camps:

11 stake-bodies—25 men in each with safety

8 coaches—possibly 5 men in each

7 pickups—10 men in each

2 ambulances

1 screen-body

8 dump trucks—could have been used, but hazardous

All but one of the vehicles were running. King received

orders from Sheldon, he said, "to oil and gas all trucks and to stand by" at 8:30 on Monday morning. He did not know why the vehicles had not, in fact, been used to evacuate the veterans when the train did not arrive.[84] King's testimony clearly contradicted that of Sheldon. From the vehicles King listed, it would seem that at least four hundred veterans might have been evacuated, even if the dump trucks had not been used.

A truck driver from Camp 1 testified that he had asked King for the keys to a truck so that he could "take some women and children out, but he refused." The truck driver did not, however, "hold Mr. King responsible because he told me the reason for his holding the keys was that he might be called on by Mr. Sheldon to use the trucks at any time to get the men out." He also testified that "at least 90 percent of the men" were capable of driving the trucks, adding: "I understand that Mr. Sheldon said they were too drunk to drive out but that is a gross mistake. . . . I was not drunk and others were not drunk."[85] A mechanic in charge of the trucks in Camp 1 likewise testified that King had the keys and that "there were not over twenty men drunk. It was after pay day and most of us were broke by then. There were plenty of men killed there that do not even drink and they could have driven out the trucks and taken every man out of here."[86]

A veteran at Camp 3 was asked if anyone had prohibited or discouraged the veterans from leaving the camp before the storm, and he replied: "No sir. They took all the keys out of the trucks." He had tried to find a key at 5:00 P.M. on Monday, when the hurricane was beginning to tear at the camp, but the keys had been collected. He testified that there were "about fifteen or twenty trucks, sufficient to have removed all of the men at camp."[87]

The assistant auditor for the camps, Wilbur E. Jones, testified that he was away from the camp but returned on Sunday at Cutler's request. He said that nobody else at the camp headquarters was as concerned as he and Cutler and one or two others. Cutler had attempted to get a train ordered, but Ghent had insisted on letting Sheldon handle all arrangements. The inquiry then proceeded:

Q. What did Mr. Sheldon do when he came back?

A. I believe Mr. Sheldon did nothing Sunday other than look at the barometer.

Q. Did he ask the advice or opinion of any of you people there?

A. No, not to my knowledge.

Q. Did anyone tell him what you people thought and what had been done in his absence?

A. No, not to my knowledge.

Q. Why didn't they?

A. My honest opinion is that I thought Mr. Sheldon was the type that wouldn't listen to anybody else, and would do what he wanted to, and what I could say would have no effect, and therefore, I would probably be better off if I just kept my opinion to myself.

Q. Was Mr. Sheldon a hard person to approach?

A. No.

Q. Was he arrogant, dictatorial?

A. Somewhat, I would say.

Q. Is that the reason people would hestitate to speak freely to him?

A. That was my reason.

The interrogation then proceeded to the day of the hurricane:

Q. What were they doing around headquarters Monday morning?

A. Nothing of any consequence.

Q. Nobody was preparing for the storm in any way.

A. I think that Good said something to Mr. Sheldon about making preparations for the storm. I am not sure that the response was too enthusiastic.

Q. Did any of the fellows play poker Monday morning.

A. Yes, they did.

Q. Did Mr. Sheldon take part in the game?

A. It was just a penny ante poker game and there was nothing doing and they were playing poker.

Q. There wasn't anything to do? There seemed to be plenty to do. Isn't that right?

A. I don't know what you mean. I didn't like to voice an opinion whether there was plenty to do or not.

Q. If you thought conditions were alarming, there was quite a bit to do?

A. Yes, quite a lot.

. . .

Q. Did you have any motor transportation at your camps?

A. Yes sir.

Q. How much?

A. I don't know.

Q. Well, just a rough idea. How many people could you have taken out?

A. This is a guess. With every available vehicle, we could have perhaps handled between three and four hundred.

Q. Did you have any drivers?

A. Yes.

Q. There were enough administrative employees to drive, wasn't there?

A. No, but perhaps enough other drivers.

Q. Was anything said about this motor transportation?

A. Not a word. Except that two veterans asked King, who was the Transportation Head, if they couldn't get a car and take one of the veteran's families out, and he couldn't give him orders to do that.

. . .

Q. Was anything said by Sheldon about taking the motor transportation out to safeguard it? Don't you think some of that time he used playing poker might have been used thinking of these things?

A. I don't know. I think a little too much stress is put on that poker game.

. . .

Q. Did Mr. Cutler do anything to prevent the sale of beer or ale at the canteen while Mr. Sheldon was away?

A. Yes, he closed the canteens and Mr. Sheldon opened them up on Monday.

Jones told the investigators that if Cutler had been in charge, "I think Mr. Cutler would have come through and probably gotten the men out."[88]

Another member of the staff confirmed that Sheldon was not an easy man to advise. Sheldon's attitude, he told investigators, was

one of what might be called second nature knowledge on every subject which could possibly be brought up in his presence. From the day he arrived at the veterans camps as Assistant Director in charge of the three camps on the Keys he attempted to leave the impression with all the members of the staff that they knew absolutely nothing concerning the camps that was unknown to him. Veterans' camps being a new thing and my having been with those camps since their beginning I felt as did other members of the staff that there were a great many things about which Mr. Sheldon should know before giving definite orders about things which he knew nothing of but I found that advice or constructive criticism was definitely out of order and it seemed that in every case when we men who knew what should be done made the proper suggestions to Mr. Sheldon we were never allowed to even finish stating the suggestion much less being asked for advice as to what orders should be given and how those orders should be carried out. Taken all in all Mr. Sheldon was very much out of place as acting head of the veteran's camp.[89]

Sam Cutler, Works Director, and second in command

under Sheldon, agreed that Sheldon "didn't welcome suggestions from others."[90]

According to John Dombrauski, the head mechanic at
Camp 3, King came to the camp at 3:00 P.M. on Monday and
said: "Where is Colonel Sheeran? Let's get the drivers and
trucks and move all we can." Dombrauski asked Colonel
Sheeran for the keys, but Sheeran said: "No, let them stand
where they are." King, too, asked for the keys, but got the
same answer. He continued: "We got uneasy about four
o'clock. Roofs began coming out. It began taking the place
down. Some of the drivers were getting ready to steal
the keys. Colonel Sheeran sent his bookkeeper, Sergeant
Mushow, to stick by the keys. We were going to steal the
trucks and go out with them." Sheeran, he said, had
refused to free the trucks because he was convinced that
the train was coming and that they had plenty of time to
get out. Dombrauski said that the trucks were in "A-1
shape," that they could have had all the drivers they
needed for the trucks in three or four minutes, and "if
Colonel Sheeran had given us those trucks I believe we
could have gotten every man out," even leaving as late as
5:30 P.M.[91] Sheeran had supervision of all trucks connected
with the bridge project. An attendant at the camp filling
station also confirmed that there were plenty of trucks and
drivers.[92]

When the civilian officials of the camps surveyed the
veterans, they later testified, all they could see was drunks.
Eugene Pattison, field engineer for the FERA at the camps,
told investigators that the "trucks were in shape, but I
doubt if you could have found that many drivers to drive
them," because "the men were drunk." He claimed that
"you couldn't have rounded up enough drivers of the
trucks . . . and I was down in camp at four o'clock Sunday
afternoon, and there wasn't two men in Camp Number 3
sober."[93] This, of course, did not necessarily apply the following day, Monday, when evacuation by truck seemed
called for. The great preponderance of veteran testimony

already quoted clearly contradicts the testimony of officials. A waiter in the Camp 1 mess hall also recalled that
there had been "very little" drinking at the camp on the
day of the storm.[94]

CONCLUSIONS

From the conflicting testimony of officials, other civilians,
and the veterans, some conclusions can be reached. Cor-
roboration from many sources indicates that a combina-
tion of camp vehicles and bridge project motor transport
was probably adequate to evacuate all of the veterans in
one trip, at most in two, to the town of Homestead. Their
prospects of surviving the hurricane there were certainly
better than on the exposed keys. This being the case,
Ghent's rejection of this alternative as impractical because
there was not "a sufficient number of trucks" is incompre-
hensible, even given his isolation from the camps. Even
more shocking, however, is Sheldon's testimony that there
were only "six trucks" and they were "not in first-class
shape." This was so greatly at variance with the testimony
of his own director of transportation, truck drivers, me-
chanics, and other veterans that it is difficult to believe
that Sheldon could be so uninformed about the transport in
his own camps.

Testimony that Sheldon had, in fact, ordered the trucks
readied and fueled Monday morning for possible evacuation of the veterans would seem to indicate that the camp
director was not as ignorant of the real situation as his testimony would indicate. More likely, Sheldon was trying to
justify his decision to place all of his reliance on the train
by his statement that there were insufficient trucks. Perhaps Sheldon, disturbed by his inability to make contact
with Ghent to obtain authorization for the train, was con-
sidering the use of trucks if Ghent could not be reached.

Once the train was ordered, Sheldon would have made Ghent look foolish had the train arrived on the keys to find empty camps. In ordering the train, Ghent and Sheldon had gambled everything on the ability of the train to arrive on time. Sheldon knew that the train was on its way; he could only hope that it would arrive in time.

Clearly, the veterans should have been evacuated earlier. The presence of the storm in the Caribbean, the unpredictability of past hurricanes, the vulnerable condition of the veterans' camps on the keys, and the visible precautions being taken by "locals" all around them should have dictated that the personnel of the camps be evacuated on the Key West-to-Miami train Sunday afternoon, which had been augmented especially for the purpose of evacuating the veterans. Failing that, Ghent or Sheldon should have ordered the train back to the keys once it had reached Miami. To wait until the ravages of the hurricane were imminent would have shown incredibly poor judgment under better circumstances, but to expect that a train could be assembled within a reasonable time on a holiday weekend was especially foolhardy and, as it turned out, fatal.

Shipped to the camps by a Roosevelt administration eager to avoid incidents in Washington, the veterans were placed at the mercy of the elements on exposed keys, in flimsy shacks and tents during hurricane season, under administrators who were inexperienced in hurricanes, indecisive, and unresponsive to advice, who thought they could plot the hurricane and evacuate the men only when the camps were in imminent danger. All around the camps, preparations were being made for the storm, and even within the camps those who were familiar with hurricanes were taking measures to protect the equipment used on the bridge project. But despite the urging of those who had experienced hurricanes and others who took such warnings seriously, Sheldon and Ghent did not move until it was too late. Sheldon's phone call on Monday, even if it had reached Ghent, would have placed the train at the camps an hour and a half earlier than it reached them, at best, which probably would not have permitted the evacuation of all three camps before the hurricane struck. But by waiting until the last minute, Sheldon would be courting disaster if he could not immediately reach Ghent for authorization. And Ghent, by his lighthearted failure to provide his hotel with a number at which he could be reached during that critical hour and a half, guaranteed that disaster. Ghent and Sheldon put all their faith in the train they had ordered too late and denied the veterans any other options for themselves.

The separation of authority within the camps between the Works Division and the Camps Division undoubtedly worked to the detriment of the veterans when the hurricane arrived. On September 1 and 2 the Works Division was headed by men experienced in hurricanes, the Camps Division was not. The Works Division secured its equipment in advance of the hurricane and housed its civilian employees (and a few veterans who came aboard) safely on dredges through the storm. It had no authority over the veterans. As one of the construction employees put it:

Somebody should have been placed in charge. Somebody familiar with the surrounding country. It was all up to the Camp Commanders. If it had been construction camp solely we could have carried them up the road to safety. The men had never been through a hurricane before. The officials in charge of the camp did not know anything about it and were not informed that it was as serious as it was. They did not give it a thought, did not take it seriously enough. If you go through two or three of them you will take it seriously. If you take precaution you are safe and if you do not you are not.[95]

The veterans of World War I were about to fight one last battle, needlessly, thousands of miles and more than fifteen years removed from the trenches of Europe.

Chapter 3

The Dead

Shipped from Washington, stranded only slightly above sea level on the Florida Keys with scant natural protection and only flimsy shacks and tents to cling to, the veterans waited in the path of a hurricane for the train that would arrive too late. The hurricane winds would demolish their pitiful man-made shelters and convert the building materials into deadly projectiles reminiscent of the shrapnel and machine-gun bullets they had faced in France. As they clung to whatever they could to brace against the winds, a tidal wave estimated at fifteen to twenty feet swept over the keys, clearing them of the last traces of their camps, drowning many of the men, and carrying others to a watery death at sea.

The man in charge of the construction work at Camp 3 testified that the cabins built to house the veterans had never been intended to withstand hurricanes and that they were not, in fact, as strong as the houses of the civilian occupants of the keys.[1] A veteran testified that "they were supposed to block up the shanties but the way they were blocked it was suicide for hurricane weather. They had sawed off trees into blocks 1½ or 2 feet long and set them on top of the ground and then the house set on these. For bracing they nailed boards down the sides of the shanties onto the blocks—that was awful." He had, he said, "laid there many a night knowing that it would be like a match box if a storm hit." Whoever was to blame for constructing the shanties in this way, he said, should be investigated.[2] A veteran from Camp 5 testified that the men were living in tents, with water on both sides and nothing to hang onto. "That is all I can tell you," he told the investigators, "except there were 183 men in that camp, besides the ones on pass, and there are only 32 or 33 of us here now, and the rest were washed away in the waves."[3]

The accounts of the survivors told of the vulnerable situation in which they had been left by the policies of the Roosevelt administration in Washington and the incompetence of their officials in Florida. Some of the accounts that follow were taken from newspaper interviews. The greater share of them came from statements by survivors taken by government investigators in the weeks following the hurricane. In interviewing the veterans, the government investigators were primarily interested in determining any responsibility for the tragic loss of life and in identifying the names of the dead and the survivors. They were not interested in hearing the experiences of the veterans during the hurricane itself, and most veterans interviewed did not describe their experiences, while others were interrupted by the interviewers when they began to do so. However, enough veterans did manage to tell their stories to enable the reconstruction of the horrors they experienced. Most of the accounts are from camps 1 and 3, since there were so few survivors from Camp 5.

CAMP 1

One survivor of Camp 1 told a reporter his story from the hospital, where he was recovering from broken ribs, a mashed foot, a back injury and numerous cuts and bruises:

We had received warning of the approaching storm and were told a train was on its way to take us out. About 5 o'clock in the afternoon the captain came into the mess hall and told us to hurry as the train was due any minute. It was already blowing hard then and we piled out as fast as we could. As we came out of the door the corners of the mess hall started breaking off and it began blowing harder each minute and by the time we got to the railroad tracks it hit us with all its force. The canteen blew down and wood started flying in all directions. It was terrible. The rain slashed and the wind kept knocking us down. Darkness came all of a sudden and I found myself lying between the hard road and the tracks trying desperately to hang on for my life. I and Scanlon, my buddy, were together holding fast to a rock. Then the tide came up and we thought sure we would drown. We were washed all over the road and finally managed to get hold of a telephone pole. Buddies all around us were shouting in panic. "Give me a hand, buddy. Save me, I'm drowning"—and other shouting in panic. These were mingled with the groans from men already too far gone to cry aloud. I fought hard to keep my head out of water and inch by inch managed to creep to higher ground, where I found another pole. I took my belt off and strapped myself to it. After what seemed eternity I heard a swishing noise, then a shriek and realized I had been hit by flying debris. I learned later it was the roof of the barracks that had fallen on my chest. A barrage of stones kept hitting me all over the body and then I partly lost consciousness. I hung on through the night in a semi-dazed condition and when day-break came I could see the bodies of my dead comrades all around me. It was a night of horror.

The medical officer at Camp 1 was also brought to the hospital suffering from numerous cuts, bruises and abrasions. He told reporters:

The storm started in fury at 8 P.M. A lot of people were washed away and others left dead after the storm passed. One man I talked with counted 80 dead persons at this camp [No. 1], and the total probably will be from 125 to 150. Every building was razed and at one time the tide rose entirely over the island.

I was at Snake Creek Hotel, which was used as a hospital. This collapsed about 10 P.M., with many persons under the ruins. There were about 40 patients in this building, about half women and children. Out of this number there were only seven men and three or four of the women and children saved.

When the building toppled over, I was able to walk through a hole in the wall into about three or four feet of water filled with floating timbers and debris. The wind was about 50 or 60 miles an hour and carried flying timbers that caused most of the casualties.

With the aid of a flashlight I made my way in the direction of the railroad grade, which was the highest point. I reached a high bank covered with grass after walking about 150 yards and being knocked down numerous times by flying timbers. I finally reached a rock wall about four feet high where, with a bunch of other men, I huddled another 20 or 30 minutes.

When we found the water still rising, we made our way to the railroad track. Placing ourselves behind the grade, we dug holes into the earth under the cross ties, so we could protect our heads from flying debris. This was the only way we could find to keep our brains from being crushed out. We stayed on the railroad track until 3 A.M., as that was the only point above water.

At daybreak Tuesday we found a tank car full of water which offered refuge from the wind and a number of others built a fire and made coffee for the sick and injured. There we remained until late in the afternoon, when we were rescued.

He added that the medical director of the camps was killed in the collapse of the Snake Creek Hotel.

One survivor described how he was swept out to sea by the tidal wave when the cabin in which he and his friends were living was torn from its foundation:

The storm struck us about dark. The train got there but went by to the lower camps. It tried to return but we understand it over-turned in a washout. . . . Had the train reached us early in the afternoon, it could have returned with those from our camp.

During the storm I was in a cabin which didn't last 20 minutes. The shack went to sea and I and my friends with it. Four of us kicked out the windows and began swimming in open water. Fortunately a shift in the wind brought us back to shore, we spent the night clinging to a coral reef. Later we took refuge behind a water tank car which was heavy enough to withstand the wind.

Many others were washed out to sea and failed to make their way back. With the speed and fury with which the storm struck, it didn't take long to clean up everything in sight.

I'd a whole lot rather be on the battlefield amid the machine gun fire than go through such a storm again. In a battle there's always the chance the enemy has bad aim. Anyway a person can shoot back. In a situation like the one I have just gone through, a man could do little or nothing for himself.

Another survivor from Camp 1 said, "It was awful—awful—how we got out of it alive 1 don't know." He continued:

We got the first radio message about 9:30 [A.M.]. They said there was a storm coming. We didn't suppose it would be so bad, and didn't do anything about it. Then a little after noon we got another report—that a real hurricane was coming.

We were told the train would get there about 4 P.M.—and told to get ready to leave. We waited—and the storm got worse and worse. There was timber flying through the air—and the water got higher. When it seemed like the whole camp was going to be washed away—we saw the train coming.

Some of the camp men flagged it—I think they got on. It went on—we never saw it again.

It was like something that just couldn't have happened—but it did. There was a big wall of water—15 feet high—20, maybe. It swept over those shacks and messed them up like they were match boxes. We hung on the best way we could—to railroad ties and trees—but most of us got washed against the reefs.

He had bruised legs, a mashed chest, and a badly cut neck.

Another Camp 1 veteran, with crushed bones and countless lacerations, told his story in whispers, broken by sobs:

I swam around—couldn't get very far—just kept myself and another guy up. Then a building washed on top of us—I had to let him go to save myself—I saw him washed away—oh, it was horrible—I tried to get us both out.

He broke into tears and could not go on. A visitor at Camp 1 described his own experience:

You can't imagine how sudden—and how awful it was. At noon we were told to expect a storm—maybe a bad one—but that a train would arrive in time to take us out.

We packed up in the afternoon, and assembled, ready to leave—but the storm hit before the train got there. When it did, I guess it was about 8 P.M.—and it was pitch black and blowing like fury.

I saw bodies with tree stumps smashed through their chests— heads blown off—twisted arms and legs, torn off by flying timber that cut like big knives.

When the train came I was hanging to the [railroad] elevation—and dug into the sand to keep from being blown away. I saw the sea creep up the railroad elevation like it was climbing a stairway.

The train went on through—heading for the other camps on Lower Matecumbe. Then, some time later, we saw it returning— I don't know just when—but we could see the headlights about two miles away. Then the lights disappeared.

A veteran recalled:

The skipper ordered us all in when we got the second warning, shortly after noon, that a bad hurricane was coming. If we'd known that in the morning, surely we could have got away.

All the storm seemed to come at once. There was a bad wind—but then suddenly things seemed to break loose—the cabins—timber—trees—shells and rocks. They might have been bullets, the way they cut through the air.

I think the fact that the sea swept clear over the key and there wasn't anything to hang on to was what made most of the boys lose their lives.

Another Camp 1 veteran said:

Four other boys and I were sitting around in the camp discussing the storm. . . . We'd been telling ourselves how much better this was than France. I guess we shouldn't have been bragging. The next minute we were under water. I guess a mountainous wave hit us. We were carried across the road to the west side of the railroad track.

Three of the group then disappeared.

I saw a big beam swish through the air and hit Jimmy Conway in the back of the head. He dropped as if a shell had hit him. I crawled along the lee side of railroad fill to a tank-car. I clung to the platform railing. It seemed like a lifetime. I found out later it was only 15 hours. I could hear people screaming for help, but I didn't dare leave. I tried to outshout the howling wind and direct them to the car. Ever so often I'd succeed and another person would join me. There were about 30 of us clinging there half-drowned. At last, when the storm let up a little bit, we fought our way to the south end of the Snake Creek embankment. We were ferried across a couple at a time and were loaded in a truck.[4]

Another Camp 1 veteran:

On Monday, September 2nd, Labor Day, before noon, I asked our captain about the storm, and if it was dangerous; he said he thought it would be; and I asked him if he thought there was going to be any transportation out of there. He told me if anything threatened, that the train would be ordered. Along in the afternoon again I asked him, and he told me same, that he was expecting the train any time. Then about five o'clock, I guess it was, I asked him again; but in the meantime, though, he ordered us all to pack our suitcases; and be ready for the train. Around five o'clock, or nearly five, I asked him the third time about it, if there was going to be a way out of there; told him if there wasn't, I wanted to get away myself. So he said he was expecting a train any time. Well, then, he assembled us all, sounded the siren, assembled us all in the mess hall, and about a quarter past six, just a little later, because a fellow asked me what time it was, and it was a quarter past six; a little later than that; of course at the same time the wind was getting stronger, then it really came, tar paper and lumber and timber and paper and so on was flying. Well, I left the mess hall and went over into a rock quarry, which was a private concern, not the one which I worked in at Snake Creek; a private concern, where you could climb down and go in. So then about—a fellow asked me what time it was again; there was about eight of us laying there in the rock quarry; and it was quarter till seven. . . . Still raining. I suppose it was probably five minutes, or maybe ten minutes, we were all excited, we were watching the boom there in the rock quarry that lifts rocks, and the one that does the lifting—not the upright—the ones that does the lifting, buckled—bent up, you know; that caused the guy wire that held the boom, to drop down across the telephone wires and railroad. Well, the train came along then in a few minutes; as I said before, it was quarter to seven; probably five or ten minutes after that; at that time it was raining very hard, and the wind blowing; the train whistled just once. Well, somebody, I don't remember who it was, said, "Let's run for the train," so we did; some of us went up and down, falling over one another, the wind blowing and so on; anyway, all of us made the train there; and I suppose the train laid there, I would imagine, 20 minutes. But in the meantime though, that wire had came down from the boom, went between the cars and the engine; couldn't pull the train; that pulled this boom down through—I don't know what you call that boom, I suppose you would call it—they pulled that down, that is how we happened to catch the train. Then we of course was on the train, the train started again, and we went out right on to the post office at Islamorada; of course we didn't know at the time where we were, because you couldn't see it; the windows were all broke out, water coming through the train, and so on. Well, we stayed in there until the next morning.[5]

Another veteran recalled:

Some dared to go out of the shacks for food around supper time, but it was hard to get ahead with the flying objects around. One fellow did get a can of soup. When we seen how terrible it was getting, we took his word for it. I thought I could miss a meal or two. Still, by that time we'd got orders to wait for the train. . . . I had no idea there was danger like what we went through. I guess it was about 8:30 when the shanty got picked up by water . . . turned up . . . and all of a sudden—CRASH! The only thing I remember is that a blanket and a mattress fell over my shoulders—it probably saved my life. I heard a crash and felt my head—then I felt myself fading away, like soaring into space, floating, floating. . . . I don't know how long that was. When I come to I was "puking"—and I looked up and there was lumber around me and I was pinned in. I struck my hand out to see how I had to climb out—[6]

At this point the interviewer interrupted.
  Another Camp 1 veteran testified:

I went up to the shack and hung around and I was ready for the train, my baggage, and we just stayed around and stayed around and finally I saw a roof blow off, I saw the roof blow off the supply house and I said we better get out and just then the shack just started to crack and so we got out and leaned against the shack and it gave another crack and we dropped everything and started out from the shack and we went to the flag pole, the flag pole had a concrete base about one foot in diameter and about three of us got holt of it and tried to get our heads behind it to protect them and our feet were sticking out and the rocks hit us everywhere and we said we better go over to the rock quarry so I had a hat on and pulled it down as far as I could and we had a road like this one out front so we started out on the road on our stomachs crawling and two of my buddies left me and so that left me by myself and the wind blew me over about three times and I got over to the quarry and stayed there all night long but as far as the train I heard the whistle blow but it was blowing and raining so hard that I couldn't see very much but the train went by; as far as time we had plenty of time. . . .If we had known the train was not coming we could have found dandy places to stay but when the shacks started to blow down we couldn't get out.

Asked in a subsequent interview how the camps might have better prepared if they had known the train would not arrive, this veteran testified that they could have used the trucks and that they could have protected themselves against the wind and rain by holding on to some heavy machinery about a block away. Of his experiences, he added,

I was in the shacks and we could see these big wash tubs flying through the air. . . . I could hear the boys all around hollering and screaming and I could hear the shacks crack. Of course, all the wires were down then and I was waiting for daylight and finally daylight came and there were a couple of buddies besides me. I walked round some . . . and the bodies were lying all over the roadway and lumber piled on them and some of them had holes in their heads.[7]

Another Camp 1 veteran recalled:

I was in the barracks. We had eaten about 5:00 P.M. and as soon as we ate I went to the barracks. I was going to go fishing and was monkeying around the shack getting things ready. I generally fished about two hours after supper most every night. On that evening it was raining and I was waiting for the rain to stop. It kept raining more and more and the wind was blowing. The wind kept blowing harder and harder and began shaking the shack and things like toilet articles and mirrors began falling. I got nervous. There were four of us in the shack and we all went out together. . . . The shack started moving around and I looked out and saw the roof blow off the mess shack and I saw boys running across the street. There was a train across the way and they were trying to get to that train or something. I do not know whether it was the train that had come down or just some cars there. I know I saw a couple of cars there and all the boys were headed that way. Our shack got to moving around too much and we went out. As soon as we stepped out the water was up to here (motions across just below ribs) and I do not know where it came from. We could not face the wind—it was too strong—we had to go around the shack. We were all together leaning against the shack and holding to each other. I heard William Clark holler that the roof was coming down. We all started away in the same direction and the roof came down on us. It must have hit every one of us. After the roof fell all I could hear was the grunting and groaning of the boys. I never saw any of them after that. I remember struggling under the roof and I could feel it dragging over my back—the wind was blowing so hard and I was under the water—and finally I got out. I got from under that wreck some way and I tried to get up and every time I got up something would hit me and push me down. Finally I got hold of a beam that was drifting around with the wreckage. I held on to that and another beam came around and I was caught between them. That is how I was hurt. I ducked under and got away from the beams and then got hold of a part of a roof and held on to that. I was floating around and could feel myself going up and down. That part of the roof washed up against some brush and trees along the shore and I stayed on it until morning. The next morning I called for help for about two hours and no one came around. I crawled to the road and lay there until noon before I saw any one. Some of the boys were coming around there from all over. They were making a fire across the track but I could not get to it. One fellow finally got me a wet blanket and I lay there until about 6:00 P.M. Then they brought me in a row boat.[8]

A veteran who worked at the Camp 1 infirmary recalled:

The storm was approaching the afternoon of the 2nd and the Captain got out the sandwiches; may have been 3:45 or 4 o'clock. Went in and had sandwiches and went out to my shack which was way down on the end. I got in there and the storm kept increasing; the wind was blowing pretty strong at four o'clock, getting pretty rough. I went to my shack and I was standing in the door looking and the storm kept increasing. First thing I noticed was the front end of that supply room where they kept clothing and such material, the end of that started to cave in first. May have been around I would say five o'clock because I could see; it was yet daylight. The storm kept getting worse and worse and the trees standing around my shack began popping. Commenced to get dusk then and the wind something terrific. I looked beyond the hospital, there was a new shack where the men who were working in the hospital slept and I saw that thing picked up in the air like some giant hand had it and whirled through the air. I thought to myself this won't do at all. I went around to where they had an aquarium and had a little low house. Could not get in it. Men standing. . . . Limbs breaking down. I said, "I will get out of here." Another fellow came up and he said, "you better come in this little house here; that will stand the storm better than any." I went there; it was then dark. There were five of us in there. Could not see anything. We stayed in there till it got so hard and the wind looked like it had switched around then. About 8 o'clock this tidal wave hit that house and turned it over three or four times; I don't know how many times, could not say. I thought we were going to get killed because there was a big cable weighed 1,800 to 2,000 pounds and on a great spool. I said if that thing ever fell on anyone, he is a goner. Finally when I got out of that thing, the water was so severe and you could not stand up, the wind blowed so hard you could not stand without holding on to something. The building next to this house had collapsed and I was holding on to one and the siding came down over nearly half the house and hit me on the chest and stomach. I was already ruptured there once before and busted out at that top. . . . And hit me in here. I was down under that thing straining and trying to get out from under the water which went over my head. I thought I was gone. The water receded quick and I was on one of the high spots of the island. I thought what it must be like in some of the low places. When that water receded, I thought I was half-drowned. Spit it out of my mouth and you could not look toward that storm at all; it would gouge your eyes out. Lot of stuff in my eyes anyway. Even your ears blistered where the sand and wind peeled the skin off. The reason I got my eyes in such a fix, I kept trying to look to see if I saw a house or something coming, so I could keep clear. I could not see a thing. In the meantime when I was pinned under this thing and when I was straining and trying to get it up, it began to slide off; if it had not been for that, I would have been gone. I didn't know what to do. I could hear it creaking and groaning. I didn't know what time would be my last. Could not see anything. Finally I just sat down on a kind of big bush and I know I must have stayed there till about three in the morning. There was a tank sitting on the side of the railroad—happened to put it in there the morning. . . . About ten thousand gallons of water. That is the only thing that stayed. They kept hollering; I could not tell the direction but could just hear. Finally about three o'clock I could see something, some kind of an old flashlight nearly burned out. I crawled to that. Had to hold to the grass, rocks and finally made it. When I got there, seven or eight people right there. One of them was a lady and she is the one that had crawled down the track about a quarter of a mile when that wind started. She was there and another lady. I don't know who she was. I got to the other side of that tank and the wind just howled and howled and kept right on till daylight and still howling. . . . They commenced to come from different places to this tank. This was eight or nine o'clock in the morning. Finally practically everybody left in camp around there was there and stayed there all that day until about three next morning before I could get away.[9]

A veteran from another camp, who was in Camp 1 working on the camp newspaper, wrote:

I was in one of the cabins near the water line at Camp #1 when the tidal wave came. Apparently the cabin was moved out into the water. The water began to fill in very fast to the extent that some of the boys were strangled, including myself. About the time we had given up hope apparently a shoreward wave brought us back to the shore and we felt the cabin hit on the solid beach. We immediately escaped from the cabin but I cannot say whether or not all the occupants escaped due to the confusion and darkness. Following my escape from the cabin and crawling with the help of anything I could get hold to anything else I could hold of, I was struck by two timbers on the shoulder and arm. I was caught between these timbers at the time but I managed to pull my arm out from between them. Following that, I was struck with rocks, etc., from time to time until I reached the top of the hill and the road. From that time I don't recall anything that happened for some hours. I finally managed to crawl to what was formerly a building and found a small improvised hole under some lumber. I remained there during the balance of the night. About daylight next morning, I attempted to get out from under this lumber and finally succeeded. I walked up to the road where Capt. Hardaker, Superintendent of Camp #1 and a group of men were standing. Capt. Hardaker found a bottle of beer and gave it to me and arranged that I have a mattress and a blanket to rest on. I remained in this position until aid came from the Coast Guard, Red Cross, Legion and others.[10]

This veteran's right arm was broken in two places, his right shoulder was bruised, his ribs were crushed on both sides, and he had a dozen prominent cuts and bruises on his body. When interviewed, his right arm and entire torso was encased in a plaster cast.

CAMP 3

The survival of veterans at Camp 3 can be attributed to a considerable extent to the presence of a tank car filled with water, which had arrived only a few hours before the storm. The veteran in charge of the fresh water supply at the camp described the circumstances under which the tank car was there and still full of water:

At noon, approximately at noon, a car of fresh water containing ten thousand gallons was placed on our siding. I . . . went to Colonel Sheeran and informed him of the fact that the car of water had arrived. After discussion, it was decided best not to pump the car into our storage tanks; in the event that the storm was disastrous, there would be sufficient supply of fresh water on hand. Incidentally, the failure to pump this car resulted in the saving of some fifty lives. At least fifty men were saved by clinging to this car during the storm.[11]

Paul Pugh, top sergeant at Camp 3, described his own ordeal and his debt to the tank car:

At 5:00 P.M. Monday, we noticed the first stiffening of the winds. The men ran for the mess hall, which rocked and tottered as the wind increased. The wind roared so we could barely hear each other speak.

Suddenly, at 7:00 P.M., the roof of the mess hall went flying off into space. The men scattered, most of them seeking safety on the railroad embankment which rises sheerly. Others sought shelter in huts and other buildings, which began crashing around us.

About 70 men grabbed a water tank car. The wind gained in fury and it seemed seven thousand hells had broken loose. At the same time, the water started rising. We could see it creeping up the bank.

It was hell to just hang on and not be able to do anything. When we were in France, we had something to fight against. Down here, we just had to wait for death and do nothing.

Hard-bitten men, who have known all the rough edges of life, who hadn't thought of God in years, prayed that night. I heard them mumbling prayers as they held to the car and tracks, with a howling wind driving particles of sand into them and debris pelting them.

Suddenly, the hurricane puffed harder and blew up the tracks, men holding them were thrown back in the tangle of whirlpools and debris. Almost at the same time, the tidal wave rushed over the tracks, tumbling men back into the mangroves where they were battered to death.

We on the tank car just held on, with our hands raw from the strain. The water rose higher and higher and finally covered the tank car, but we held on just the same.

Then the wind stopped, the stars came out and it seemed that the most wonderful thing in the world was happening. It was just a lull. It lasted about 40 minutes. Then it really started blowing.

Finally, morning came—and the light never looked so good. The wind slowed down and the water receded. We looked around and only 70 men hanging on the car were to be seen. We thought all the rest were dead.

From over in the wreckage of mangroves, however, we heard a terrific yell. In a moment someone answered and soon there were hoots back and forth. Many of the men swept from the embankment had washed over in the mangroves and then clung to the top of the trees while the tidal wave tugged at them.

The men were torn, bruised and nearly wrecked physically, but their spirits were fine. They took it like the men they are. They all say they'd rather go through five wars than another hurricane and I feel the same way.

There's one thing we'll always remember—that's good old tank car No. 3390. That's the one we hung to. If it hadn't been full of water it would have blown over too, but when the tracks on each side blew up it just sank a bit and held fast. We held fast too and we love it like a mother. I'll never see a tank car without wanting to pat it lovingly. . . . It's only a miracle anyone is alive. I doubt if we'll ever know just how many are dead.[12]

The superintendent of Camp 3, B. E. Davis, recalled:

At 6:00 P.M. the hurricane hit us with high winds blowing in gusts gradually increasing in intensity. Around 7:00 P.M. the roof blew off the mess hall. I instructed the men to leave and to make their way to safety. Most of them went to Bradford's Store. At 7:30 P.M. [the] roof left Bradford's store and the men were again forced to seek shelter wherever they could, but were advised to take the other side of the railroad track, some getting in and around automobiles and rode the first storm through. The water was 12 or 14 inches deep running like a river over the camp. The wind velocity had at least reached 150 miles an hour. All the buildings were gone by this time and we had a casualty list of two dead and a small number wounded by flying debris. At 9:00 P.M. we had a calm which lasted 55 minutes. Having been in a hurricane before I knew that the storm was not over and would return from the opposite direction, so we collected and decided to board the beer boat and the ferry boat in front of the camp and the Panama dredge boat in back of the camp, also the water tank car located approximately one-half mile below damp. These were our only objects for safety. I told the men that it was every body for himself and to keep cool heads, that I was going to the water tank below the camp and the men who chose to go with me to follow. On the tank car we could hear the rustle of the water in the ocean, which sounded like the rustle of leaves but as it came closer it came in with a deepening roar. At 10:00 P.M. I watched the water coming in on us from the top of the water car. It was at least 25 feet high and completely submerged us with approximately 5 feet of water. This, with a terrible wind behind. This was practically the worst part of the storm. Men were washed from the track as the track was completely torn down and turned over by the water, and the men on the tank were saved by the track falling against the side of the car. This is where our greatest loss of life took place. We survivors were helpless to help one another. At 6:00 A.M., daybreak, we proceeded to get off the tank car and to rescue the injured; 3 men being pinioned between the track and the water tank were released, 2 living.[13]

A civilian employee at Camp 3, secretary to Colonel Sheeran, testified:

On Monday barometer readings were fluctuating. . . . I talked to Col. Sheeran personally Monday concerning this and asked him if he knew anything about the men getting out. He said that he had tried to prevail upon them the necessity of moving the men and it was now up to them. Between two and three o-clock I was informed that the train was enroute. I asked the colonel if I should board her. He said "It is best that you do so." I then went to my shack in which 4 other men were billeted. We packed and were in readiness for the train. In the meantime the storm was upon us and gathering terrific momentum. This was between 4:30 and 5:00 P.M. Monday but I will not swear to this. We could hear the shacks turning and lumber being thrown against the shacks. And, sand and rain became so violent that it turned our shack over completely and it rolled until it hit another shack ending in an upside down position. I broke the screen out of the top of a window and peered out and suggested to the other fellows that we abandon the shack and go out the top side, which we did. When we got out two of us swam until we reached a tree and protected our heads from flying timber. The lull then came and at 7:30 there were so many dead and hurt the boys suggested that I contact Col. Sheeran to take charge. I swam and waded about 200 feet to calling distance to him. It was impossible for him to get to me but he hollered that that was just one half of the storm and we should seek a high place. I transmitted this information to all and we went up the railroad tracks, about 70 of the other men hanging on a tank car. I proceeded up the track along with a good many other boys. The first wave that came off the railroad turned over and carried us off. I grabbed a telephone wire while swimming and it broke. I then swam some more, grabbed a limb, straddled it for about an hour and it broke. Then I landed on top of a limb that held me until 7:30 the following morning. I approximate the time the wave picked me up at about 9:10 because all the watches of the boys who were drowned stopped at such hour. When I was able to get my bearings the next morning I saw approximately 8 men who came out alive with me. I was then carried to a house boat and given coffee and soup and remained there until 3:39 Wednesday afternoon when we were transferred to Miami by yacht. If the train had arrived and the men had attempted to board same during the terrible storm many men would have been killed and injured in my opinion.[14]

A veteran who served as timekeeper at Camp 3 recalled:

I was in the Camp. Was in my shack at the time the first blow started about six o'clock, it was a very terrific blow. Our shack was one of the few that held up during the first blow. About fifteen men were in that shack. After the first blow was over it got very calm, the stars came out and there was no wind at all. About thirty or forty minutes later the second blow came with a tidal wave. Most of the men made for the water tank down on the railroad tracks, and I believe there were about one hundred men congregated down there when the tidal wave struck. A good many of them were washed off into the mangroves, and I was one of the ones who were washed off in there. As soon as day-

light came so we could see I found there was three other men
hanging on besides myself. We had to jump into the water and
swim about thirty yards back to where the trucks used to be and
we found many men there congregated around that tank. It
rained and blew pretty hard all day Tuesday. Captain Davis
asked me to check up on the number of men who were left and
still in camp, which I did. They check up as 136 living at the time
and 36 dead men which we helped take out of the mangroves
and the water.[15]

Another Camp 3 veteran testified:

All I could say is that when the ferry boat arrived about four
o'clock [Sunday] and we were having chow and she was warned
not to leave, that the hurricane was on its way, and what we read
in the papers and heard in Miami about the hurricane coming, so
Monday at four we had to go down to mess hall to get sandwiches and in about fifteen minutes we got orders to pack up our
clothes and stay there until we got word the train was there. We
just stood there and stood there and the wind kept blowing
harder and harder and all I can remember is a shack going over
and it blowed me about sixty feet and I grabbed the beam of the
shack and I was in water until about thirty minutes later until
the storm let up and Captain Davis told us to go on the [tank car]
and there were about forty in front of it and I saw them go and of
course we couldn't [help them and] save our own lives and in
little while the tidal wave broke my hands loose from my hold
on the bottom of the tank and threw me into the woods and I
thought I was going into the Atlantic but I could swim [and] that
saved me. I swam until I found a tree big enough to hold me and
I set there all night and then the boys started hollering "you"
"you" to find out how many were in there and then we waited
on the tree until the storm was pretty well over. I suffered so
from the cold and then when I got out I went to the boys on the
tank and one man was lying by the tank dead and something was
wrong with his leg and some died that couldn't get out of the
woods and we started to picking up the bodies.[16]

A kitchen worker at Camp 3 testified:

Well, I was working in the kitchen the day of the storm, and it was about eight o'clock in the morning I went over to Bradford's, the fellow that ran the store, to get a bottle of beer. While I was drinking the bottle of beer there was eight or ten in there. I don't know who they were, I didn't pay no attention; and there was a fisherman came in, and he says that the barometer is falling; he says "We are going to have a hurricane here some time today"; that is what he said. . . . And somebody else says "When is the storm going to land here?" Well he says "I don't know, but it will be some time tonight." So that is the first time I heard there was anything about a storm or a hurricane coming. So I went back to the kitchen, and we got dinner, and we give them dinner, and they was all talking about the storm; but nobody was excited. Somebody says it was 24 hours before it would hit us, some says 10; and they had it all figured out, and I was under the impression, somebody said there was a train at Homestead to take us out; that is 40 miles from there. . . . I don't know who; everybody was talking. . . . Well we started to get supper; they had dinner and went back to work, and we started to get supper. And about two o'clock somebody come over and says that there will be no supper, you better make sandwiches instead of giving them regular supper. . . . So I didn't get supper, we put out the stove, and we started to make sandwiches. We made two sandwiches apiece, and a couple of pots of coffee. Then we waited until four o'clock; this train was supposed to be in there, all the time. . . . So we had all the sandwiches made, and we decided to feed them at four o'clock instead of waiting until five. . . . So we started feeding them. . . . So we went in the commissary, and [they] wanted to put stuff on the train so we would have it to eat; they claimed we was going to Hollywood, Florida. We got all the stuff out, we put sardines and all canned stuff and put it in a pile; got our clothes and brought them over in the mess hall; and by that time I guess it was about four-thirty, and the wind was blowing pretty hard then, and everybody started coming in the mess hall. And we were all kidding about the storm was going to land, and the train would be there sure by five; put the train back another hour; said the train would be there by five o'clock. . . . We stood around there and kidded; and the wind was blowing harder all the time; and we stayed there I guess until six o'clock; and the wind was sure blowing them. And I guess it was about 6:15 the top of the mess hall went; there was about seventy-five in the mess hall then. The top of the mess hall went off, and we all had to move, so everybody started to run; and I run over in back of the railroad track and I laid down over there; and Smith the mess sergeant was with me, and a fellow named Diamond. . . . and a fellow named Lyons; there was four of us. We all set over at the back of the railroad track. And the telephone pole started to blow down; well, we thought that was charged with electricity, and we didn't want to get electrocuted, so we gets up out of there, went to stand up; and the shack started coming over, so we had to lay down again; it was either get your head knocked off by a little shack, or get electrocuted; so we said we would take a chance on getting electrocuted, but it happened to be there was no electricity in the wires. We stood there until that storm was over, but that was the first one. After that we got up on the railroad track, and Blackie Pugh had a flashlight, he was the only one had a light; it was dark then; and we got everybody together we could, and he said the best thing we can do is to find a higher spot here, the tide might come in. Well, there was a water tank up the railroad track about two hundred yards, or three hundred yards, I guess; well, he says that ought to be the high spot where that tank is. We got to the tank, I guess it must have [had] seventy-five at that time, we all got together, we got to this water tank. And somebody came up with a lantern and says, "We better look over the railroad track and see how high the water is." . . . So he looks over the bank at the water, and the water was right at the edge of the railroad track. Well, he says, "Here we go, we either got to swim or do something, that water is coming up fast." And about five minutes, the water did come over and everybody made a scramble for this tank. I guess there was seventy of us got on it, on just one little water tank; it was loaded with water; and I don't know how many got washed off; there was about seventy of us got on anyhow, at first, And the railroad tracks alongside of it started over, and went up against this tank; it stood there, didn't move no farther than the tank, or didn't knock the tank off the track;

we were still on the tank. And we stayed there until morning. It was about nine o'clock when we went on the tank. The tide kept coming over the top of this water tank.[17]

Another veteran told investigators:

We waited, and there was no train come; and about six o'clock we was all ordered into Bradford's place; some went to the mess hall, and some went around; I myself was in Mr. Bradford's place; it was packed in there with me. That is when the first wind started blowing real hard. And a bunch of fellows come running to the door and tried to get in Bradford's; they said the mess hall was blown down. And at that time something began hitting Bradford's place, and it wasn't very long until that roof come in. I got out of there and into a man named Kelly, his shack; and as soon as we got in there it blowed down. I ran outside, everybody was running, you couldn't see nothing; I got picked up and throwed to the ground, that's where I hurt this arm; I got throwed down again on top of another chap, and we laid there until the first blow was over; after that she calmed down, something about three quarters of an hour, I guess, maybe an hour, I am not sure. A bunch of us made it up toward the water tank; I got on top of that tank, and some more fellows got on it; it was dark and I couldn't see who they were. I don't know long it was, she started blowing again, I don't know how long; then the water started coming over; kept blowing until daylight. The water came and then the water went back. Some fellows were really blown off, or let loose, or something, I don't know.[18]

Another kitchen worker in the camp recalled:

We were right on the lower keys; lower Matecumbe. They came back and told us boys we had nothing to worry about; that there was nothing to worry about . . . until eight o'clock the next morning anyway, if we got it, but we might not even get this— that is, the full blast of the hurricane. So then Captain Davis gave orders for us not to get a regular dinner, to make sandwiches.

. . . We made cheese sandwiches and weenie sandwiches; we made a sandwich for everybody, and didn't serve a regular meal. Then the next order we got, the train would be there at 5:00. By that time the wind was blowing I judge from a 40 to 50 mile gale; the small trees was bending right over and the rain was terrific. And it began to get worse, and we had our rations ready to load on the train, by the door, and there was about 20 or 30 of us in the mess hall waiting for the train. Then the captain give orders not to try to load anything, the minute the train got there to jump on it, just to get ourselves on and never mind anything else; but they still said we had nothing to worry about. The train was to be there at 5:00, then 5:30. No train; and it began to get worse and worse; it would have been impossible to have even got out by motor or any other way, it was too late, and I think some of us began to realize it was too late; I did for one, realized that we was in it, from what I had heard, and heard the fishermen, since I had been down there the eight months. And about between six and six-thirty, our mess hall went in, went in, right from the center; that was the first. Of course, our roof blew off first, and it was a crash, nearly everybody ran just like a bunch of rabbits; and when we ran out, we ran right into that wind; and after that I don't remember much what happened to the boys, because the wind knocked me right on the bannister of the mess hall, and I hit the ground, and I got up, and it knocked me down three times before I stayed down; then I began crawling, because the timbers and pieces were flying from those shacks and buildings, and one of the boys that had that piece stuck through him, was right in front of me, the piece passed by me. I got behind the railroad track in the first storm, and I hugged that track as long as I could, up to the bank, until after the first was over; then I suppose it lasted, this terrific wind lasted for perhaps an hour, I don't know, but I didn't have any way of telling; and it quieted down just like that, just stopped, and the stars come up and the wind seemed to get warm, and it was just as still, a piece of paper wouldn't flutter in the air. But then we began to all huddle together, naturally, and it was a fisherman come by and he told us, he says, "Boys, find a place. . . . This is right in the middle of it, and it will be back," he said. "Whatever you do, don't go back where that lumber is laying piled and strewn, it is very dangerous; I think the best place would be up this way." So we walked up the track I suppose between a half—not quite half a mile from our camp, and we had a water car up there, a tank car—a regular oil tank car, but we had it filled with water, which had been dropped off that morning; and we all huddled around that car. I suppose it was 100 or maybe more of us, we got around that car during the lull. And when the wind came again, we could hear, twenty minutes before the wind hit, we could hear that roar, it began to roar in your ears just like a far away rumble, that wind and water, and the water, when it came over just like that, and we began to mount the car. We got up on the car, and they were all around the car, that is where we lost most of our boys that was washed away, or blown off the car, that couldn't hold; some of them perhaps jumped off when the car began to go over—we thought it was going over, several of the boys leaped from the car and were drowned and killed that way. I remained on the car all night; until daylight the next morning. I was right up on top of the car.[19]

A first aid attendant from Camp 3 described the circumstances of what the *Miami Daily News* described as "the most hideous single fatality of the tragedy at Camp 3":

We were expecting a train to come. We was told to pack the ambulance with emergency dressings and dressings which we might need and the ambulance would then go up the road and they wanted to take someone out of camp to go with the driver and I suggested I go with the driver and they said, no, they wanted me to go on the train. We got the ambulance packed and the men ready to drive and they said, "Let's go over to the store." A man named Bradford had a little store. We goes over to the store waiting for the train. Pretty soon the wind started blowing; it had been blowing before but pretty soon it started, I mean blowing. . . . Must have been around five o'clock. The ceiling of the store came down on one end and the other end standing up and everyone rushed for the door. I was amongst them. Just as I got outside the door I was struck in the back of the head with what I think, was the filling station pump. I went out and when I come to myself I was in an automobile and someone rolled up the glass. Then the wind let up kind of and they told me the ambulance driver was hurt; could I do anything for him. I got out of the car, still kind of dizzy. He had a piece of timber stuck in him, protruding out. I tried to pull it out. . . . I had some dope I put in my pocket for such an occasion. I gave him a dose of pyraldehyde. I waited for it to take effect and he was begging to go to the hospital. I did not know at that time the road was washed out so I told some of the boys—could see the headlights of the ambulance—I called some of them to carry him to the ambulance and they told me one of the shacks was turned over against the ambulance. I said to get about twenty men and see if they could roll it off. Finally they told me they could not get the ambulance. We picked the man up and put him on a stretcher and put him on a truck and dropped the curtains and turned the truck toward the wind and then they hollered better go to the water tank as it was turning back [the storm]. That is the railroad water tank. I gave the man another dose of dope and then I went to the water tank and just got there and a wave was coming in and I could not get on to the tank, all filled. I grabbed hold of the rail on the side and pretty soon something crashed me and everything else taken away. I landed in a bush and stayed there till morning, three hundred yards away.[20]

The man with the stake through him died the next morning.
Another veteran told investigators:

I was out in the open when she started blowing and about 50 feet from the mess hall. I saw the crowd driving for the mess hall and I picked out a big mangrove tree. I was in the tree for something like 12 hours. It was in the neighborhood of five o'clock and we were about ready to go in and get some sandwiches. All rations were packed up and they were issuing sandwiches. I guess there were in the neighborhood of 75 men in the mess hall waiting for a bite to eat when the roof crashed in. I crawled on my stomach over to the mangrove tree which was about a foot in diameter and I put in the night right there, riding that tree up and down with the rise and fall of the water and keeping my head out of it.

Somehow with the flying debris that the wind carried there, I got hit in the back with something that seemed to paralyze me for a second. I almost lost my grip but I hung on. There were a few hours of time that I can't recall because the next I knew it was daylight and the storm was over.[21]

CAMP 5

A veteran from Camp 5 in the hospital with spine injuries told how he had seen his wife, two daughters, and two grandchildren killed before his eyes after they had reached Camp 1 seeking shelter.

Upon hearing the storm warning, I started out in an automobile from my home half way between Camps 5 and 3 with my wife, Frieda, and my two daughters. . . . We were accompanied by my two grandchildren, . . . age 2½, and . . . one year.

After traveling through increasing winds and over wreckage strewn roads for 18 miles on a flat tire, we reached Camp No. 1. We were assisted on the trip by Mr. King, of King's filling station.

The building we were placed in at Camp 1 lasted only an hour. I tried to make a human chain from the building to the railroad track to get all the women and children to safety, but I was washed out into the gulf by a high wave. I swam back as quickly as I could and reached shore just as the hospital collapsed. I heard my wife calling my name, but I was not able to get to her in time. Members of my family were all killed under the ruins.

R. Baker from Camp 5, who also took refuge at Camp 1, was killed. Another woman that I know at Camp 1 was killed, although I succeeded in rescuing her child from the waves. The survivors then took refuge behind the tank car until rescuers arrived.

Of 185 men carried on the roster at Camp 5, only twelve were found alive—four who had fled to Camp 3 and eight who had clung to trees. A Camp 5 survivor told reporters there was "not so much as a piece of two by four timber left" of the camp. He added:

I was at the camp when the storm struck. We all gathered in the mess hall. The roof left. We ran to the cabins. The roofs of these left too. The roofs left all the buildings and we climbed to the railroad embankment.

The salt water came bubbling up over this and swept the men right over the island into the gulf. I climbed a tree and hung on, with the water whipping at me.

A few of the boys did the same. The others all were lost. I doubt if they'll ever find the bodies as they were carried into the gulf. It was different than in Camp No. 3, where the bodies were wedged in mangrove and under debris.

As I was hanging on a rail before taking to the woods I saw 25 or 30 men washed from the embankment.

One of the few Camp 5 survivors related a tale of pain:

There isn't a whole piece of timber left at No. 5. Everything is twisted and torn beyond recognition. About 60 of the boys were loaded into trucks and they headed north, nothing has been heard of them since. A party of us headed down toward No. 3 but were caught by the storm, some managed to cling to trees and things. Others were swept bodily out to sea.

I made for the railroad [track] and hung on to it. A heavy sea came along and washed it up and as it settled back down it pinioned my left leg under it. After lying there for what seemed countless ages, suffering horrible agony, I decided to try to cut my foot off, but I couldn't get to my penknife.

After that I passed out. Finally I regained consciousness. I was being washed away, somewhere, I don't know where. I was thrown upon a tree. It was a mangrove. I clutched it frantically, and waited hours until daylight.

My foot was paining me terribly. Many bones in it were crushed. I started hobbling and crawling in the direction of the camp. At last assistance came and we managed to get there.[22]

Asked by an investigator what conditions were like in the camp before the storm broke, another Camp 5 veteran replied:

We were in a trap, where the camps were placed, and it was pretty bad. The Gulf on one side and about 35 feet to the railroad tracks and the camps were in between. There were 196 men in our camp and about 51 are left, in the hospital, and all told. . . . I was shipped out of Washington, August 9, 1935 and 21 men came in my camp with me from Washington and I am the only one left.[23]

The time keeper at Camp 5, who was not there during the storm, described conditions there and what he had heard from survivors:

The Food Supply building was drawn up by engineers to be "storm proof"—the pillars were buried three feet and fastened with cement. It had double floors and triple braced on top. The top blew off after every other building in Camp 5 had gone over the railroad. After the top went off the building Hill tells me he climbed up as high as he could and then jumped and the first wave caught him and carried him approximately forty yards; he caught only a pole and when he looked back the building was being washed toward the railroad and it stayed in shape approximately 15 seconds when it went to pieces and Hill and the men were trapped inside and were washed away with it. He said the wind then caught the building and carried it back into the ocean at least thirty yards from the place where it was stationed, at which time the building went to pieces—building and men with next wave went over island entirely. Hill said that the pole on which he was carried southwest from Camp #1 was carried 1½ miles away and he caught onto another telephone pole and as he was on this pole a woman washed by and he caught her by the dress and tried to save her, but as the pole was washed away he was compelled to let the woman go and she was drowned.[24]

Another Camp 5 veteran testified that he survived by fleeing that camp for Camp 3:

We were notified that there was going to be a storm Monday morning, by a camp director, Mr. Robinson; and around between one and two o'clock we got orders to pack up; that there was going to be a train in there and take us out of there at five o'clock. Well, I stayed in the camp until it was 4:15, and I seen that there was no protection, which we didn't have in there, because I helped brace these tents up my own self, and I know there was no protection for any of us there. Mr. Thompson and I got out on the highway.

Q. Were these tents or shacks?

A. Tents with roofs put on them; canvas covers with roofs on them; but there was no support. Mr. Davis taken I and Thompson into No. 3, and I had only been in 3 about 30 minutes before the storm started; then I was in Taylor's shack during the storm. There was no train in sight anyway. Mr. Davis had told us there would be one at five. We went to this shack, we went through the first storm, and then after we came out, there was no orders for trucks or anything else, we couldn't get out of there, it was just a death trap; one truck in camp, and a pick-up truck; one stake body and one pick-up. After we came out of the first storm, we were there in front of Mr. Bradford's place, and we all made for the tank car in No. 3, and there was a little supply sergeant out of 3, had a chest of cigarettes he brought up; he says, "If it does come, we will have cigarettes": he said, "there they are," and set them up on the tank car, and I got up on the chest, and he was on the right side of me, and a sponge boy from the dredge boat was in front of me; he was frightened, he didn't know what to do, so he asked me what was he going to do; and I told him I didn't know, I thought we would have to do the best we could for our own selves. And by that time the tidal wave came in on the car, and taken this little supply sergeant from my right side, and the boy that was sitting in front of me, that I had my left arm around; and just for a minute my mind was blank, I don't know whether I went down or up, but when my mind came back, and when I had hold of the running board of the tank car with my right hand, and I had another buddy along side of me, in the hair by my left hand, and I threw the guy on top of my car, pulling him on my right arm, and holding him until they pulled on me and got us up.[25]

Another veteran weathered the storm in Camp 5. The first sergeant of the camp, he said:

came around Monday afternoon around 2:00 P.M. and told us to pack up, that there would be a train down to get us at 3:30. Everybody stay in the camp and there was nothing to be worried about. . . . So about 3:30 he came around again and said the train would be there at 4:30. We were all in the mess hall at the time he made that statement. By that time the storm had started. It was blowing a pretty good gale at that time. So most of us went back to our tents and in a minute the mess hall blew over. Some of the men were killed in there but the most of us got out of there and went back to our own tents. The tops began to blow off of those. We was running wild, didn't know where to go. In fact, there wasn't anywhere to go. All that saved me and two other fellows was a septic tank built there which was not in use at the time. It hadn't been fully completed. About thirty of us got in that. The top of it was made of two inch boards. We stayed in there approximately two hours and there was a sewage drain from the tank to the ocean. When the tide came up, the water backed into that tank until we had to get out. The wind was blowing pretty bad. There was only a small hole about two feet square to get out of there. The water was up to our waist at that time. We all finally got out. I taken two other fellows and went over and got in the top of this tree and stayed there about eight hours. The rest of the fellows that was in there went to the highest point, which was the railroad track. At least, that is where they started. I don't know where they got to, whether they got there or not. After that I don't know what happened. All I could hear was fellows hollering, begging for help and praying. We couldn't help them.[26]

Another Camp 5 veteran also described the shelter in the septic tank:

Sergeant at Camp No. 5—Buck—he told us to pack up our personal property. He told us in the morning that we were to leave at 12:00. That is all I heard the first time. That was Monday morning. He came in again at 12:00, we were getting sandwiches for our dinner. All the dishes were packed up ready to be taken to the train. A little while after 12:00, after we had had the sandwiches we went back to our shacks. In a little while he came around to the shacks and told us in each tent to pack up our personal property as we were leaving at 2:30 on the train. So I packed up my personal property. We waited there and waited and did not know what to do, whether to go away or wait for the train. Some of the boys said what was the use of leaving there as a train was coming to take us away. We waited until 4:30 that afternoon. At 4:30 we hadn't heard anything from the locomotive coming to take us away so we just kept on waiting for a train. Around 5:00 a big storm that you could hear miles away like big machinery going around, the wind was blowing so fast. It just rained a second or two and then stopped at that time. Just about 5:00 it commenced raining harder and the clouds were coming from both directions and we were right there in the middle. We commenced to get excited and there was no train and so we just naturally could not do anything but stand in the shanties. . . . Just like summer tents, screened in and just piling driven in for foundations, and screened. We let the blinds down over the screens before the storm came in an effort to save the tents. We tried to save ourselves too, at the same time. We thought it was just a little storm—we didn't know much about storms then. . . . I thought it was going to be just a little storm. I picked up a paper and saw it was so many miles away and I was scared then, so I said we would just have to wait for the train. It started really raining bad after a while. All of our tents just shook and cracked and pulled out of the nails and pilings. When it got so bad a bunch of us got out of the soaked tents—there was a cement cess-pool with three holes in it about 4½ feet high or maybe 5 feet high. So we got out of the tents and went to the cess-pool. Then the wind started blowing bad, so bad we could not talk to each other. We stopped up the escape pipe as well as we could. The pipe was going through from the cess-pool to the ocean—we packed coats and blankets in the pipe and stayed there until the water pushed the packing out, then we came out as we did not know how much water was outside and we were afraid the water coming through the sewer pipe would drown us. So about 30 of us got out of the cess-pool to keep from drowning. We came up through the trap holes and we could not hang on, the wind blew us away so fast. Some of them just hung on to each other and I grabbed a couple of men and hung on an edge of the cess-pool and we saved ourselves from blowing into the water. Finally the water was level with the cess-pool and getting higher and higher all the time. The tents were blown away and floated on top of the water. We finally grabbed on boards, floating on the water into; there was a 25-foot tree, maybe only 21 feet and I and the two guys I was holding onto went to try to climb up a little higher. We went towards the tree, a palmetto tree . . . and we climbed up it and the others . . . followed us. Three of us climbed up the palmetto tree and stayed there until next morning. Well, the water was getting higher and higher, around eight or nine feet high, some guys started hollering and praying and hollering for help. There was no one there to help us. . . . Some of the guys went over towards the railroad thinking they were high and safe on the railroad and the waves took them away. While I was in the tree I hollered to them to come up there. After a little, they were still hollering out there but in about two minutes a big wave came, it just naturally came. That was the last of the hollering I heard. It washed them across the railroad and there was no protection for them on the other side—no tree or ground, just rain and sea on that side and canal on the other side and the highway and railroad in the middle. That is the last time I saw about 30 of the men. . . . That is all I can tell you except there were 183 men in that camp, besides the ones on pass and there are only 32 or 33 of us here now and the rest were washed away in the waves.[27]

Bodies of veterans awaiting disposal. *Courtesy of the National Archives and Records Administration.*

A camp before the hurricane. *Courtesy of the National Archives and Records Administration.*

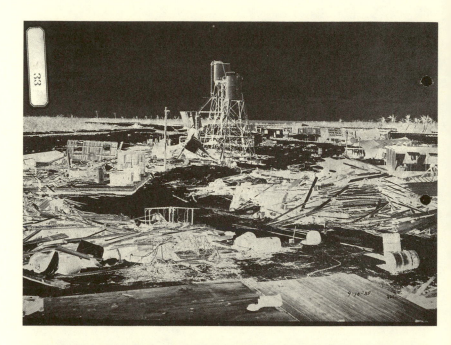

Camps after the hurricane. *Courtesy of the National Archives and Records Administration.*

A last salute to some of the dead. *Courtesy of the National Archives and Records Administration.*

A funeral pyre. *Courtesy of the National Archives and Records Administration.*

Chapter 4

The Aftermath

A few days after the tragedy, Henry Cavendish, a staff writer for the *Miami Herald*, wrote:

Hell in the form of a hurricane tore through the Florida keys Monday night and left in its wake yesterday miles of debris and desolation, hundreds of injured and dying, and other hundreds of bodies rotting in the noonday sun.

Any attempt to approximate accurately the number of dead was obviated by the scores and scores of battered bodies plastered in some places like flies in the midst of debris and littered undergrowth. . . .

The No. 1 Veterans' Camp at Quarry, just south of Snake Creek, was leveled to the ground and bodies littered the jumbled masses of wreckage round about. . . .

The Florida East Coast train which was sent down to the keys Monday to evacuate the veterans at the Nos. 1, 5, and 3 camps was located, turned over on its side, across from what was formerly the railroad station [at Islamorada]. . . .

Standing at the southern tip of Upper Matecumbe key it was possible to see where the No. 5 veterans' camp had been formerly on Lower Matecumbe key to the south. The territory was leveled almost to the ground, however; only chewed off stumps of palms and pines showing sparsely.

There were no signs of the camp which was believed to have been washed into the sea. Neither were there any signs of survivors.

Boatmen who succeeded in reaching the Lower Matecumbe waters reported seeing bodies on the shore as well as a number of bodies floating in the water. . . . Estimates of the number of dead were almost impossible to obtain, but ranged from 250 upward.

This reporter personally saw 32 bodies in the day's trek from Snake Creek to lower Matecumbe Key. . . . These estimates, however, take no account of the hundreds of persons washed and blown into the jungle debris and into the sea, of which there was no accurate possible check yesterday.

By late afternoon yesterday the bodies of the dead were in advanced stage of decomposition. They were being ferried across Snake Creek and deposited in rough pine boxes for transportation.[1]

Literary Digest wrote: "Snake Creek Hotel, serving as hospital near Veteran's Camp No. 1, crumpled as when a heavy-footed man steps on an egg-shell. Forty or fifty people were inside. A handful escaped. The total number of dead may never be known."[2] *Time* observed: "When the Red Cross, the American Legion, the National Guard and the Coast Guard finally got into the devastated Keys over the broken bridges and wrecked roads, they found signs of slaughter worse than war. Bodies were in the trees, floating in the creeks, bogged in the mud."[3] *Newsweek* added: "If a child built a tiny village of matches and paper and then aimed an electric fan and garden hose at his toy town, we would approximate the effect of last week's disaster on Upper and Lower Matecumbe Keys."[4]

A *Miami Daily News* staff writer, Henry G. Frampton, wrote of the hurricane scene:

Lower Matecumbe key, with the broken bodies of 266 storm victims strewn in its gnarled wastes of mangrove, twisted steel work and smashed concrete, today carried on the piteous tradition bequeathed it in days of yore by a vanquished Indian tribe.

Matecumbe—a name rather euphoneous to English speaking people—means, in the tongue of the ancient Calcosas: "The place of sorrow."

There the Indians made their last stand against the conquering whites and were exterminated. There too, a host of veterans of the world war made their last stand against the might of a tropical hurricane Monday night—and met a like fate.

The island today looks like a cousin of oblivion—an arena where angry gods played fitful games of tenpins with boulders the size of mountain tops.

When a *Daily News* rescue expedition in the speed yacht *Byronic* docked at the splintered, debris-strewn wreckage of the ferry slip, it seemed impossible a living thing could have survived the cause of this sight. Yet dazed men, in tatters and blood-stained bandages, limped about, still displaying the spirit that made them famous the days of Belleau Wood and the Argonne.

Lower Matecumbe, blasted into isolation when the causeway connecting it with Upper Matecumbe was hammered into nothing, housed two veteran camps, No. 3, at the extreme south end of the island, and No. 5 at the other extremity.

In No. 5, 185 veterans were on the roster. Yesterday only 12 were found alive. Hope had been held out that a party setting out for Upper Matecumbe had reached its destination, but this was disproven yesterday, giving a possible death toll of 173 for that camp.

At Camp No. 3, 243 were enrolled. Twenty-three were on furlough, leaving 220 in the camp. Yesterday, we accounted for 133 of the men, giving a death and missing toll of 87. . . .

Tales of terror and suffering were told simply by survivors, who wandered in a fog, shocked by the horror of waiting for death in the howling maw of a hurricane, pounding, spitting surf and debris that sounded more like machine gun fire as it rattled through their ranks.

Scores, hanging on for life to a railroad tank car—the only thing in Camp No. 3 to withstand the blow, told of seeing comrades tumbled to death in the swirling waters.

Yesterday, amid the scattered fragments of the camp, 45 bodies recovered from the mangrove roots and among debris were laid out, covered with stained sheets from which protruded broken limbs. Many of the victims were crushed horribly. . . .

Back in the mangroves, from which men who should be in hospitals pulled out bodies until they were forced to stop by exhaustion, battered remains of veterans are wedged in the tangle of mangrove roots.

"In one place 30 feet square, I saw 25 bodies tangled together," one veteran remarked. "We just couldn't get them in. We'll have to wait until outside help comes."[5]

Another reporter wrote:

And the veterans, those pitiable souls who have been tossed about ever since the World War. What of them, as they perished down there where death laughed in unholy glee as he prepared for his prolific harvest?

They never had a chance.

At Camp No. 1, on Windlys island, they were caught in bunkhouses which were as so much stacked wood when the wind struck with terrific force. It is a miracle that so many were saved. It seems hardly possible that men could live through all of it.

Most of those fellows, they tell me, are the old bonus army marchers, sent down here to work, chiefly because the government didn't know what else to do with them.

Since 1918—that's 17 long weary years ago—they've been drifting through this economic comedy. You've heard that they're no good, don't care to better themselves, won't work.

Perhaps that's true—I don't know. But don't forget that these men, 17 years ago, went through weeks, even months, of hell not unlike the few short hours of a tropical hurricane. If something snapped inside during the horrors of the world war; if they no longer can see the advantages of orderly striving as we know it; if they were trouble makers—just remember that they didn't get the breaks you may have had. Their minds couldn't stand up through the continued horrors of war.

I saw their bodies down there yesterday, pretty much as I had seen bodies long, long ago on the hillsides and in the trenches. And it seemed just a bit too cruel of the gods to toss those men into the path of Old Lady Death, far down in those tiny islands. But then, perhaps to many of them it may have been just another—and at last the final—cruel quip of fate.

Of Matecumbe he wrote: "The foliage literally has vanished, and the stubborn underbrush everywhere has been whipped to shreds. Sand filled the air, as well as rain and wind, taking the bark off all trees and underbrush."[6]

Ernest Hemingway came up from Key West to visit the scene of the tragedy and wrote that the keys "looked like the abandoned bed of a river where the sea had swept." He continued:

The railroad embankment was gone, and the men who had cowered behind it, and finally, when the water came, clung to the rails, were all gone with it. You could find them face down and face up in the mangroves. The biggest bunch of the dead were in the tangled, always green, but now brown, mangroves, behind the tank-cars, and the water towers. . . . They hung on there, in shelter, until the wind and the rising water carried them away. They didn't all let go at once, but only when they could hold on no longer. Then, farther on, you found them high in the trees, where the water had swept them.[7]

Another writer described the scene in the keys:

An aeroplane dropping a bomb on what was this village, and on each of the three groups of veterans encamped on the keys a few miles below, would have caused just as much havoc as the recent hurricane. It is pretty much like the scenes behind the lines after battle—on a smaller scale. Hurrying to and from the disaster area were ambulances loaded with soldiers and nurses, trucks filled with supplies and coffins, aeroplanes, sweeping low, searching for those drowned on the flooded fields. . . . Men are collecting limp, sodden forms, placing them side by side for

tagging and identification—then they are borne to the waters'
edge and put in a rowboat which is towed to the other bank
where are the empty coffins with their occupants. . . . The air
has the never-forgettable stench of humans too long dead. Men
handling them drink strong liquor, and some drink too much
when they can stand it no longer.[8]

A Florida National Guard officer reported that his men
had "boxed and shipped 108 bodies and cremated 68
bodies, all of whom were identified as members of the
Veterans' contingent on the keys." The identification of
the men as veterans was based on "personal observation,
also by identification such as pocket books, discharge certificates, medals, et cetera found on the bodies."[9] The rapid
decomposition of the bodies under the hot sun soon made it
impossible to handle them. At the urging of Florida public
health officers, Washington granted permission for the cremation of those bodies not yet recovered from the keys.[10]

The *Miami Daily News* reported:

Dr. T. S. Kennedy, state board of health district sanitary office,
joined with those urging immediate cremation.

He returned from the keys today saying he did not know how
many are dead, "but if we had any definite way of checking all
the deaths, the toll probably would be 500." The Red Cross said
today an accurate check of the dead may never be possible. . . .

Of 817 war veterans employed in bridge construction on the
keys when a death-dealing wind leveled their camps, 298 were
missing today and 144 bodies had been recovered, the Red Cross
announced. It is known definitely that 375 of the 817 veterans
are alive, but 71 of the survivors are injured. . . . The civilian
death toll is estimated at 70 by the Red Cross.[11]

The next day the Red Cross put the death toll at 446, of
which 327 were veterans dead or missing.[12] Some of the
civilians, of course, were workers at the camps and wives,
children, and even grandchildren of veterans and civilian

workers at the camps who would not have been in the path of the hurricane had the veterans not been gathered there. The fact that many of the bodies had been swept to sea and might not be recovered for days or weeks, if ever, made an exact body count impossible. Using the August 1935 payroll for the veterans as a basis, the Roosevelt administration calculated 256 deaths. Of 696 names on the August payroll, 433 were living and one had been killed by a train a few days before the hurricane. Officially, there were 121 veterans positively identified as dead, 90 missing, and 45 tentatively identified as dead.[13] This, of course, was not consistent with the testimony of the Florida National Guard officer who reported the disposal of 176 veterans' bodies by his unit alone. It seems clear, however, that veteran deaths were in excess of 250, and that the total number of deaths associated with the veterans' camps might be considerably larger.

On September 8 the *Miami Daily News* wrote:

The sun rose this morning on smouldering funeral pyres in the Florida keys, it picked out bodies hidden in the storm-swept debris from eyes of searchers, it etched dark shadows on 116 coffins at Woodlawn Park cemetery. . . . At 7 P.M. today army, navy and marine corps planes will scatter roses from the sky, their flight into Biscayne bay scheduled to inaugurate opening of memorial services in Bayfront park."[14]

The *Miami Herald* editorialized:

Tribute tonight. Special joint services at Bayfront park for the dead. Honor to the ex-soldiers. Honor now. When it is too late. Muffled drums, hymns of praise, glory for the heroes. Cheers for their deeds when they can hear not. Tears for their tragedy. Hundreds of thousands of dollars allotted by the government for relief, when relief is of no further value to them. Living, they asked in vain. Billions for others, for idle civilians. But the aging veterans were shunted down to shacks. Washington was glad to be rid of their presence. Forgotten, these bonus marchers. Forgotten when peril threatened. Now they are remembered. Now they are lauded. After they have been cremated like so much cordwood.[15]

Twenty thousand people attended the final services for the veterans, including representatives from various veterans organizations.[16]

A few days later a *Miami Daily News* reporter described the scene on Lower Matecumbe Key:

The moon was up, reaching for the tops of two forlorn pines that somehow had survived the fate of their fellows; the heavens reflected a serenity the earth belied; the waves, calm again after their death-dealing, lapped a beach strewn with debris. Tired men sweated and cursed under their breath as they lugged railroad ties and piled them in a heap near the beach; more came with other burdens more yielding but no more animate. Seventeen such burdens were placed on the pyre. Then came a hush to be followed by the quiet prayers of three clerics. A volley from rifles, taps—then the match. And all at once, the sky that had been lighted only by a tropic moon turned a red and ugly frown upon land and water. No living thing spoke or made a sound. Only the flames crackled into the silence.

It added that a total of 172 had so far been burned at Matecumbe, and it "had been necessary, where bodies were found badly tangled in undergrowth, to burn them at the spot, but no cremations have been carried out without benefit of official supervision and church or military rites where possible."[17]

Reporting that 327 veterans were dead or missing in the camps, *Newsweek* wrote:

Over the nation ran one question: "What were the veterans doing in the whirlwind's path?" Floridians knew the Roosevelt Administration had sent the men to Florida to get them out of

Washington, where they came last winter to agitate for bonus-payment. But why didn't the FERA move them from the islands after the first hurricane warning? Why was the rescue train so late? . . .

While argument raged, funeral pyres spread dim light over what was left of Matecumbe Keys.[18]

Chapter 5

The Whitewash

Now began the investigations, charges and denials. The assistant administrators of the FERA and the VA, Aubrey Williams and George Ijams, were hurriedly dispatched from Washington to conduct an investigation. From Washington, FERA administrator Harry Hopkins charged that Weather Bureau reports had been so confusing as to make it impossible to predict where the storm would hit. Therefore, Hopkins argued, camp officials in Florida had not been responsible for the failure to evacuate the veterans. Meteorologists from the Weather Bureau, however, insisted that their information had been accurate enough as to the intensity and general direction of the hurricane for three days before it hit.[1] Admiral Cary Grayson, head of the Red Cross, agreed with the Weather Bureau, saying that its forecasts had been so good that the Red Cross had had ample time to prepare for relief work.[2]

In Washington the prime concern was with avoiding any taint of responsibility for the tragedy. In a telephone conversation, Colonel Lawrence Westbrook, assistant administrator of the FERA, asked Fred Ghent, "What was our justification for putting the camps there. Could we be criticized for putting camps on the Keys?"

Ghent: Yes and no. It is a debatable question.

Westbrook: If it is debatable, we could be criticized?

Ghent: Yes.

Westbrook: On what grounds?

Ghent: Isolation.

Westbrook: You have no communication with the camps?

Ghent: We have one telegraph office out there but the facilities are not good. [They were better in Key West.]

Westbrook: What kind of work were they doing? Work that would stand up and be a credit to the Administration?

Ghent: I wouldn't like to pass on that. That is a difference of opinion.

Ghent insisted that they did not know that the storm would definitely hit the keys until about 1:00 or 1:30 Monday afternoon, and that reports had said that the hurricane was still two hundred miles away. Sheldon had told him a train was standing by ready to move, and Ghent had ordered it out at 1:30. He and Ray Sheldon had thought that the train would arrive long before the hurricane hit.[3]

A conversation on September 4 between Westbrook and Marvin McIntyre, one of Roosevelt's secretaries, reveals the concern at the White House over possible repercussions:

Mr. M.: I've been talking to Mr. Early [another Roosevelt secretary] and General Hines. The General has instruction from the President with regard to the veterans in the camps down there, about taking care of the injured and arranging about funeral services and all that. You don't mind, do you?

Mr. W.: No, not at all. I will talk to our man down there, and tell him to report to whoever the General sends down there. I just talked to him, and if you haven't heard about the situation, I'll tell you. He said he believed 300, at least, were lost. Another hundred were injured, the remainder surviving. They are evacuating these people rapidly.

Mr. M.: My God! Between us, Colonel. There is no blame that can be attached to our Administration or to your office, is there?

Mr. W.: No, it is just a catastrophe.

Mr. M.: Nobody suggested there was any undue risk, or anything?

Mr. W.: No.[4]

Another telephone conversation reveals the attitude toward the veterans held by those at headquarters.

Mr. S.: The fact of the matter is those fellows had a very bad name.

Mr. W.: Who had a bad name?

Mr. S.: The Veterans. There will be some remarks made at headquarters that we would not want to repeat over the telephone.

Mr. W.: What are they?

Mr. S.: "If the thing had to happen, it might just as well take *them.*"

Mr. W.: Who would say that?

Mr. S.: Everyone I have heard talk about the accident.[5]

A conversation on September 6 between Mr. Milford and others in Miami further revealed the concern with criticism:

Milford: How many have we lost?

Porter: Three hundred veterans. I think there will be a total of about five hundred.

Milford: Are they getting more bodies?

Forbes: Yes. That condition is terrible. . . .

Milford: Are we being blamed a lot?

Forbes: Oh, no! The *Herald* took a good shot at the train matter, but that's all.[6]

The next day, however, the neighboring *Washington Post* took the administration to task for the tragedy. In an editorial, "After the Tragedy," it wrote:

In spite of Relief Administrator Hopkins' denial that his organization was negligent in failing to evacuate the veterans on the Florida keys, there is considerable evidence to support Gov. Sholtz's conclusion that "gross carelessness somewhere" was responsible. Indeed, the negligence seems to trace far back of the hurricane to the casual policy of assembling "bonus marchers" in isolated and semi-secret concentration camps. This point we shall again take occasion to emphasize. Sympathy for the victims of this catastrophe would be pitifully misplaced if it should preclude the most serious consideration of the issue which the destruction of the Florida camps has brought to public attention.

To many Americans the first news of these camps' existence came with the horrible reports of their demolition. Contrary to its usual practice, the FERA has not publicized this enterprise. Veterans who came to Washington demanding immediate payment of the bonus have been quietly shipped to remote localities under conditions which approximate paying them not to create disturbances. Reports that the FERA has tried to shift the camps to the CCC indicate that it is not proud of this undertaking. Nor has it any reason to be. The camps were launched without any direct legislative sanction. At best they represent a surreptitious and ill-considered approach to a very difficult problem. . . .

Apparently the only reason for creating these special "rehabilitation camps" in the South was to avoid the political embarrassment of further mass lobbying for the bonus. Of course, that very fact put a premium on "trouble-making" in the camps. . . .

A policy which tends to hide these problems from public view, segregating these unfortunate veterans under conditions which hold little promise for their rehabilitation, is one in which we can find nothing to admire.[7]

Raymond Clapper, a columnist normally friendly to the Roosevelt administration, wrote that officials in Washington were "pretty sick" about the tragedy, because: "They had regarded their disposition of the bonus marchers as just about perfect."[8]

On September 13 Aubrey Williams released the report of the investigation he and George Ijams had made into the tragedy. In that report, Williams found the tragedy "indescribable." The first indication the camps had that the hurricane was moving toward the keys, he said, "was issued at 4:41 P.M. on September 2nd." Shortly after 1:30 P.M., Ghent had decided to evacuate the camp and had asked the FEC to dispatch a train to the keys. Sheldon said that he was advised the train could reach Matecumbe three hours after the request was made, and he assumed that he had at least twelve hours to evacuate the camp, based on the position and reported speed of the hurricane. The Miami terminal had, he said, received orders for the train sometime between 2:00 and 2:35 P.M., but the fact that it was Labor Day meant that time had to be spent assembling a crew and collecting coaches, delaying the departure until 4:25 P.M. Williams then described the further reasons for delay en route, resulting in the train arriving at Islamorada when the storm was already of hurricane force. Meanwhile, Sheldon had made preparations for the evacuation of the camp and the quartering of the veterans in Hollywood. He sent three small trucks to ready things at Hollywood, leaving only six at the camps, and Sheldon had decided not to try to evacuate the men by truck due to "the condition of the equipment, the available driving personnel which would be entrusted with the lives of people, and the morale of the men," all of which he thought would make a truck evacuation "extremely dangerous." Moreover, he believed that the train would arrive in plenty of time. He placed the death toll at 44 "identified dead," and 238 "missing and unidentified" dead. The report concluded that no one was at fault for the tragedy. There had been no negligence or mistaken judgment. It was, rather, the result of an "act of God."[9]

Even before the report was issued publicly, those privy to its contents and conclusions were outraged. The Greater Miami Ministerial Association was offended that God had been blamed and wrote President Roosevelt to demand further investigation of the circumstances of the tragedy. It charged:

We regard Mr. Williams' statement that this catastrophe was an "act of God" and that all was done that was humanly possible, as a deliberate attempt to whitewash known facts, ignore the inefficiency and irresponsibility of those in charge, and to appear to be a complete investigation, whereas it is known that statements and facts contrary to this report were ascertained by these investigators and known by them and not included in their report.

Among other things, the association wanted "others than the officials in charge of the camps to be interviewed in this investigation in view of the fact that indifference to their tasks and responsibilities is apparent." It also demanded that "the investigation be made to cover also the moral conditions generally obtaining and actually existing at the time of the hurricane. It is our conviction that these conditions contributed in large measure to the tragic loss of life in the case of the veterans."[10]

A Methodist minister in Daytona Beach likewise wrote Roosevelt to protest the "whitewash" of the Williams-Ijams report. He told the President:

In the first place those keys are a place of great danger in the hurricane season. There are few, if any, adequate buildings on them. As everyone knows, the veterans were quartered in shelter that could not possibly stand a severe storm, let alone a hurricane. It would have been wise to have had the veterans working elsewhere through the hurricane period.

In the second place a hurricane was in the offing days before it struck. Preparations were made in Miami to withstand it, also in other places. True, it was not definitely said that the storm would strike Matecumbe Bay, but who could foretell that? The fact that a hurricane was in the neighborhood was sufficient reason for taking those men to a place of safety. We know that at least 24 hours before the storm struck many men begged officers in charge to move the men. This shows that plenty of people knew the danger.

In the third place the men did not go to the keys until they were given assurance that a train would be ready to leave Miami at short notice in case of danger. The delay of that train in getting away from Miami and in getting down to the keys is by this time a nationwide fiasco.

It was, he concluded, "a frightful thing that these hundreds should have so cruelly perished, and that other hundreds should be disabled physically and nervously because of their dreadful experience, all because of criminal negligence somewhere along the line."[11]

The Miami post of the Veterans of Foreign Wars likewise charged that the Williams report had "whitewashed negligence and poor judgment" which had resulted in great loss of life. John J. Skillman, a member of the national council of the VFW and past commander of the Miami post, sent his own report to the national commander of the VFW. According to the *Miami Herald:*

Mr. Skillman said he would charge that Paul Pough [*sic*], commander of the Overseas Post, Veterans of Foreign Wars, at Lower Matecumbe, and a committee called on Ray Sheldon, commander of the three camps, at 6 P.M. on September 1, demanding that the veterans be taken from the keys.

Pough reported Sheldon asked them to return at 8 P.M. and told them there was no danger, Mr. Skillman said.

The veterans' committee called on Sheldon again on the morning of September 2, repeated its request for immediate evacuation, he added.

Mr. Skillman also charges that Williams only heard the positive side of the story and did not call on any of the veterans who went through the hurricane.

A sweeping denial of Skillman's charges were made later in the day by Sheldon, who declared no veterans' committee called on him.[12]

The Florida state commander of the VFW called on Roosevelt "to direct an immediate, thorough and impartial investigation to fix the responsibility for apparent negligence of those in authority, and that the negligent persons, if any, be suitably punished."[13]

When Aubrey Williams phoned Conrad Van Hyning, a Florida ERA official to ask if the situation had "quieted down," he was told: "The VFW have gone out. The ministerial group have gone to the President to make an investigation." The important thing now, he thought, was to get the veterans transferred to the CCC. Williams replied that the CCC had "agreed to take any that will meet the physical conditions. . . .It is being worked out today."[14]

The Florida Governor launched his own investigation of the tragedy, and the American Legion, likewise, appointed a committee to conduct an unbiased and impartial study of the incident.[15] Meanwhile, Harry Hopkins had now begun to try to deflect criticism by pointing out that the veterans had been sent to Florida to help the state Road Department with the Overseas Bridge Project and were, therefore, "technically in the care of the Florida relief administration."[16] This was apparently intended to absolve the Roosevelt administration of responsibility, even though it was the administration that had sent the veterans there! The report of the Florida State investigation, conducted for the governor by State Attorney G. A. Worley as hurriedly as the Williams-Ijams investigation, found no evidence of negligence.[17]

A *Miami Daily News* reporter concluded over a week after the hurricane:

Five incontrovertible facts stand out: (1) Hurricanes are destructive and dangerous. (2) This is the season for them in this part of the world. (3) Knowledge of the general whereabouts of this particular hurricane existed for several days before it struck. (4) The keys are narrow ribbons of islands, almost at ocean level, and practically without trees or other physical defenses against the elements. (5) About 600 veterans and 400 civilians were living there mostly in tents or flimsy structures.

It seems clear that no adequate plans had been previously developed for saving the inhabitants of just such an emergency. It was like building a 40-story frame hotel with no fire escapes.[18]

A few days after Harry Hopkins released a special FERA grant of $200,000 to Florida for hurricane relief work,[19] the *Miami Herald* editorialized:

They were shifted around. They marched on Washington. They asked for the bonus and were given the "bums' rush." They were a problem. Then months ago they were shunted down to the keys to work. And the hurricane solved their troubles. No more wandering and wondering for hundreds. Peace in the midst of turmoil. Sudden flash of battle, the roar of wind and rain and sea. So quiet now. Taps. . . . That tragedy south of Miami may be the final straw which will push over the bonus payment for all veterans. When a government has billions for boondoggling, aesthetic dancing, art culture, worthless canals and schemes without end, it must have funds for the defenders of the nation. . . . When $200,000 can be thrust out in a moment, after it is too late to help the dead, it ought to be possible to do something for the living.[20]

In the midst of denunciations of the government's handling of the veterans' camps and demands by national and local chapters of veterans organizations for an impartial investigation, the American Legion and VFW prepared to hold their national conventions. From New Orleans, site of the VFW convention, the national commander, James E. Van Zandt, charged that "scores of veterans who lost their lives in the Florida keys hurricane last Labor Day were sent to the key camps from Washington to forestall another bonus demonstration in the national capital." The *Miami Herald* reported:

The commander said he considered it "ironic" that veterans who had gone to Washington in behalf of the bonus had, by their deaths in the hurricane, made their own bonus certificates immediately payable.

"It is a well known fact," said Van Zandt, "that a majority of the men on the Florida keys were veterans who assembled in Washington with the hope their presence might stimulate favorable action in congress on the bonus."

"It is also well known that [Roosevelt] administration authorities were anxious to avoid a repetition of the 1932 bonus army situation and the congregation of perhaps thousands of veterans in the capital."

"As a result, veterans who arrived in Washington were given the opportunity of food, clothing and lodging in veterans' camps in Florida operated under federal emergency relief administration control under policies similar to the civilian conservation corps camps."

And there over three hundred of them had died.[21]

A few days later, Veterans Administrator Frank T. Hines revealed that the FERA had discontinued the practice of sending transient veterans from Washington to "rehabilitation" camps like the ones on the keys.[22] At the same time, four congressmen told the VFW convention that they would get their bonus shortly after Congress convened in January.[23] Columnist Ray Tucker described the hostile mood of both the VFW and the American Legion as they approached their September national conventions, writing:

The vets are enraged over the deaths of their comrades during the recent hurricane. They brand the Williams-Ijams report as a "whitewash" and have conducted their own investigations through Florida representatives. Extremists proposed condemnation of the handling of the 1935 bonus army. . . . [The Roosevelt] Administration will have defenders at both assemblages. Their backstage advice will be to go easy on criticism lest it jeopardize the political gentleman's agreement under which congress will enact the bonus next January—even over a veto.[24]

Some of the steam was removed from the veterans' pressure when the Roosevelt administration announced that the VA would conduct its own investigation of the tragedy, with a view to fixing the blame for it and determining whether there was any negligence involved.[25] This investigation, conducted by D. W. Kennamer of the VA under the direction of Colonel Frank T. Hines, administrator, aroused concern within the FERA that at least some responsibility might be attributed to that agency for the tragedy. John Abt, assistant general counsel of the FERA, who had been involved in the earlier investigation, was chary about the VA inquiry going back through the same witnesses. Aubrey Williams, assistant FERA administrator, phoned him on September 14 to explain the FERA position:

W. Kennamer said you told him you had not received any instructions to take any testimony or join with him in the investigation.

A. What I told him was that as far as the general investigation was concerned, I thought we had done everything.

W. I don't want you telling him that. That isn't our attitude at all.

A. But he wanted to start all over from the beginning.

W. What we want is to cooperate on any basis they want to work.

A. But the difficulty is he has it in his head there has been some negligence.

W. If he feels that way, let that develop. We will meet that situation in Washington.

A. It would be a terrible mistake to start going through those witnesses again.

W. We can't help that. The President is holding the General responsible for the investigation. I find here we are just cooperating
with them. They are responsible really for the investigation. I
don't want him to come up here with any doubts at all. I want him
to have an opportunity to get some records concerning his doubts.
I want you to clearly understand that we want to have you stay
and work on that basis. . . . I want you to develop a very cordial
relationship.

A. My only difficulty was I thought it would be a mistake to go
through the whole thing again.

W. But we can't say anything about that. Say whatever he wants
we want, too, and when we write the report. . . .[26]

Clearly, Williams expected that whatever Kennamer's report said, he, Harry Hopkins, and the others in the FERA
would be able to tone down any criticism of the FERA
before it reached final draft form.

For his part, Kennamer was equally reluctant to have Abt
involved in the VA investigation. He wrote to the Chief of
the VA Investigative Division, Sam Jared, Jr., that Abt had

already formed a definite opinion about the matter and if there
was any attempt whatever to whitewash the matter he was a
party to it and endless trouble will be experienced with him if we
undertake any further investigation with him and if I am to sign a
report I certainly want to question FERA employees and find out
if there have been any threats or intimidation, as there are rumors
to that effect here in Miami, that certain employees were told if
they wanted to continue to work for the state FERA they had
better be careful what they said.[27]

A few days later Kennamer reiterated that he was skeptical
about Abt's willingness to cooperate, since Abt insisted that
the facts had already been established. Kennamer, on the
other hand, was convinced that the FERA investigation had
been "incomplete and unsatisfactory," and he worried that
witnesses would not testify candidly if Abt were present.

Kennamer had already found "strong indications that pressure is being exercised somewhere along the line."[28]

Kennamer's first difficulty was in finding Ray Sheldon, who was finally located in West Palm Beach. Although Abt had earlier denied knowledge of the camp director's whereabouts, Sheldon told Kennamer that Abt and others in the FERA knew his location and phone number. At first Sheldon refused to answer questions without Abt being present, but finally responded to the few questions Kennamer asked him concerning a Jacksonville weather advisory sent out at 3:30 A.M., Monday, September 2.[29] These questions had been prompted by a wire from the VA chief investigator asking if Sheldon had received the advisory.[30]

For the remainder of September, Kennamer's team solicited new testimony and sorted through the data already obtained from the Weather Bureau and other sources. Once back in Washington, Kennamer wrote and assembled a report in three volumes for submission to VA Administrator Hines. In that report, Kennamer was considerably more critical of the handling of the emergency by the Florida ERA than was the FERA investigation. Among Kennamer's conclusions were the following:

That the weather advisories sent out by the Weather Bureau were received by officials at the Veteran's Camps and contained information that should have put them on notice to take immediate and effective steps to be ready to evacuate the camps when it became known such action would be necessary.

That the officials of the Florida East Coast Railroad cooperated with the officials of the Veteran's Camps and started a train to the camps within a reasonable time after they were notified to furnish a train.

That Captain E. H. Sheeran, Superintendent, Bridge Construction, acted prudently in taking all available steps to safeguard bridge equipment on Sunday, September 1st, before the hurricane Monday evening, September 2nd.

That Mr. Ray W. Sheldon, Assistant Director of the Camps,

should have done the following things after he returned to the camps Sunday afternoon, September 1st:

(a) Continued the instructions issued by Mr. [Sam] Cutler prohibiting the sale of beer and ale at the camp's canteens.

(b) Issued instructions for Mr. B. E. Davis, Superintendent of Camp No. 3, to return to the camps Sunday afternoon.

(c) Made definite plans Sunday evening for evacuation of the camps in the event it became necessary.

(d) Issued definite instructions to the Superintendents of the three camps to be in readiness to move on a few minutes' notice and information as to how the men would be entrained, where they would go and what equipment to take along.

(e) Telephoned Mr. [Fred] Ghent immediately after being told of the Monday 3:30 A.M. weather advisory and have insisted that he order a train to the camps immediately to wait there for the evacuation of the camps in the event it became necessary.

(f) Assumed authority to order a train after the Monday 10:00 A.M. weather advisory and have ordered a train at that time in the event he couldn't get one ordered by a person who had authority to order a train.

(g) Gotten the motor equipment in readiness to move the men out in the event a train could not be obtained. . . .

That Mr. F. B. Ghent, Director of Veterans' Camps for the State of Florida, should have done the following things:

(a) Completed an arrangement with the Florida East Coast Railroad for this road to furnish a train on short notice in the event one was needed to evacuate the camps located on the Florida Keys, and have advised his assistant of such an arrangement weeks before this hurricane.

(b) Completed arrangements for a train to be in readiness to go to the camps immediately after his telephone conversation with Mr. Sheldon at 5:00 A.M. Sunday, September 1st, and have advised Mr. Sheldon of this arrangement and the details as to how this train would be ordered.

(c) Kept in frequent communication with the camps Sunday and Monday, September 1st and 2nd.

(d) Kept himself available to the telephone and the Telephone Company advised as to where he could be located at all times from Sunday morning, September 1st, through Monday morning, September 2nd.

(e) Communicated with Mr. Conrad Van Hyning, State Administrator, and kept him informed as to what was being done to safeguard the lives of the veterans.

That Mr. Conrad Van Hyning, State Administrator, Florida Emergency Relief Administration, should have done the following things:

(a) Required Mr. Ghent to complete arrangements with the Florida East Coast Railroad to furnish a train in the event one was needed, weeks before this hurricane occurred.

(b) Communicated with Mr. Ghent from time to time after he knew about the hurricane and have known that he was taking proper steps to safeguard the lives of the veterans.[31]

Clearly, in Kennamer's view, Sheldon and Ghent deserved more than a little blame for their contribution to the consequences of the "act of God." But, as Williams had assured Abt in September, the FERA now set out to emasculate Kennamer's report.

Through November and December the report underwent many alterations as a result of the efforts of the FERA's Williams, Hopkins, and Abt. Memoranda of those months indicate that the conclusions were being redrafted.[32]

Abt's conclusions based on the Kennamer-Abt, VA-FERA joint investigation were apparently forwarded to the VA in January 1936.[33] Colonel George E. Ijams of the VA, who had been involved in the first VA-FERA investigation, found Abt's insistence that the Florida ERA officials were blameless untenable, writing that "Colonel Sheeran's actions, along with other evidence of danger, should have caused the responsible officials to make definite arrangements to be ready to move the men in the event the danger became imminent." Sheldon's insistence on doing nothing until the danger was imminent, Ijams wrote, meant that by the time he was ready to take action it would be too late. He concluded,

The evidence is clear that definite arrangements should have been made for the evacuation immediately after the 10:00 A.M. advisory, Sunday, September 1st. It appears that after the 3:30 A.M. advisory, September 2nd, the train should have been ordered to the camps; that after the 10:00 A.M. advisory steps should have been taken to entrain the men, and that after the 1:30 P.M. advisory they should have started away from the camps.

In this and other conclusions, Ijams was in agreement with Kennamer. The VA's representatives in both joint VA-FERA investigations both blamed Shelton and Ghent for the delays that resulted in the deaths of the veterans on the keys.[34]

In forwarding Ijams's response to the Abt report to FERA Administrator Harry Hopkins, VA Administrator Hines concluded that "it is practically impossible to agree entirely on all the points at issue, and it is my suggestion that you and I send the two reports to the President with a covering memorandum."[35]

Instead, what apparently happened was that Kennamer and Abt were instructed to agree on a joint "statement of facts" concerning the Florida tragedy. A few weeks after Hines forwarded to Hopkins the Ijams memorandum, Aubrey Williams's FERA office borrowed the VA copy of the Abt report and the statement of facts agreed to by Abt and Kennamer, and the documents were not returned. Kennamer had agreed to the joint "statement of facts" only on condition that it be accompanied by his "general comment." In a memorandum of June 23, 1936, Kennamer described this background to his "general comment" and placed it in the files. In his "general comment," Kennamer wrote:

The evidence is undisputed that on June 6, 1935, Mr. Ghent had been put on notice by the co-receiver of the railroad that the railroad would require 12 hours notice to place a train at the camps; that it would be necessary for the officials who had charge of the veteran's camps to make prior arrangements for detraining the veterans at whatever point they were to be taken and to advise the officials of the railroad of such arrangements, in order that the railroad might make necessary arrangements for taking care of the equipment and the train crew after the train arrived at its destination. The evidence is also clear that the arrangements demanded by the railroad were not made and that the railroad was not notified of the point to which the veterans were to be taken until the order was placed for the train. Therefore, with these facts undisputed it must be concluded that no prior agreement had been made with the railroad; that the railroad by proper authority and to the proper authority had notified the Florida Emergency Relief Administration it would require twelve hours' notice to place a train at the camps and actually placed the train at the camps in less than six hours' time after it was ordered, and would have placed a train at the camps in much less time if it had not been for an unforeseen obstruction across the railroad track. With these facts completely established it must be concluded that the railroad officials cooperated with the officials of the Florida Emergency Relief Administration and are not in any way culpable.

As for the Florida ERA, Kennamer wrote:

Sound administration and prudent precaution demanded prior arrangements which would not fail to get the veterans out of the area in the event of danger. This was more mandatory than would ordinarily exist had the camps in question been located at many other places because the Florida Keys are long narrow islands only a few feet above sea level and means of escape were very limited and the veterans were almost wholly dependent upon the F.E.R.A. to take them to a place of safety and there were practically no places of refuge from danger occasioned by hurricanes on the Keys. The only extenuating circumstance for Mr. Ghent's failure to complete definite arrangements for evacuation of the camps is his testimony to the effect that his letters to the National Emrgency Relief Administration at Washington regarding this matter were unanswered.

Thus, the FERA in Washington was linked directly to the failure of the administrators to get the veterans off the keys before the hurricane struck.

Kennamer wrote further:

The poor judgment used by Mr. Sheldon was his failure to be ready to move when it became apparent this would be necessary. . . . The evidence is conclusive that no time should have been lost getting ready to move after the 10:00 A.M. advisory, Sunday, September 1st; that part of the readiness to move should have included a definite agreement with the railroad to furnish a train; that this agreement should have been made by officials of the F.E.R.A. and railroad who had authority to make such agreement and that the agreement should not have been a vague understanding that a train could be furnished at such and such a notice, but should have been an agreement that the railroad would furnish a train upon a given notice and by whom the train would be ordered. . . . If the purpose was to delay evacuation of the camps until it was definitely known that the area would be in danger from the hurricane, the train should have been brought to the camps immediately after the 10:00 A.M. advisory [September 2] and waited there until it was definitely known that it would be necessary to evacuate the camps. This statement is not based upon second guessing because the evidence is conclusive that Mr. Cutler would have gotten the men out much earlier had he had the authority. The evidence is also conclusive that

Colonel Sheeran would have taken action to get the men out had he had the authority. It is only necessary to contrast what Mr. Sheldon and Mr. Ghent did with what Mr. Cutler, Colonel Sheeran and Mr. Duncan did to establish that Mr. Ghent and Mr. Sheldon did not take the action prudent men would have taken.

Kennamer concluded his "general comment" by writing:

In finding that Mr. Van Hyning, Mr. Ghent and Mr. Sheldon failed to do many things prudent persons would have done, the Investigator is aware that three reports of investigations have already been made, one by Mr. Howard P. McFarlane, one by Captain Watson B. Miller, both representatives of the American Legion, and one by Colonel Aubrey Williams and Colonel George E. Ijams, and understands that the reports submitted by Mr. McFarlane and Colonel Williams and Colonel Ijams exculpates these officials and that the one by Captain Miller fails to find them culpable. However, the Investigator is also aware of the fact that the persons who submitted these reports did not have all the evidence contained in this report and that some of them were not in a position to obtain all the evidence. He also appreciates the fact that reasonable men may honestly differ about this matter and that there is no evidence whatever that any of the officials referred to intentionally neglected their duties. With the unrefuted facts that no definite arrangements were made for a train after the 10:00 A.M. weather advisory Sunday, September 1st; that no train was kept waiting at the camps as early as possible after the 10:00 A.M. weather advisory, Monday, September 2nd; that Mr. Ghent and Mr. Sheldon did not communicate with each other from 4:50 P.M. Sunday afternoon until 1:37 P.M., Monday afternoon; that Mr. Ghent and Mr. Van Hyning did not communicate with each other at any time from August 31st through September 2nd; that Mr. Ghent did not keep long-distance advised as to where he could be reached at all times Monday morning, September 2nd, and that it took one hour and fifty-five minutes to get him on the phone when he was much needed, he can not find that they did all the things they should have done or all the things demanded of them by nature of their respective positions.[36]

Despite considerable ballyhoo in the newspapers over its initial investigation, the American Legion report on the tragedy was never released, perhaps because the approaching vote on the bonus bill made it seem impolitic to that organization. The legion's report was, however, sent to President Roosevelt by Ray Murphy, national commander, on November 2, 1935.[37] Roosevelt sent the report on to Hopkins, with a note: "Will you and General Hines talk this over and let me know what you think we should reply to Ray Murphy?"[38] Hines wrote to Hopkins in mid-November:

I have read this report and it will be my purpose, of course, to discuss it with you at such time as the mutual discussion of reports on this same subject by the Federal Emergency Relief Administration and the Veteran's Administration has made the necessary progress. This should be soon. In the meantime, I believe the President should acknowledge the submission to him from the American Legion.[39]

There is no copy of the American Legion report in either the VA or FERA files, nor is there any evidence in those files or in the Roosevelt papers at Hyde Park that any reports on the Florida tragedy were submitted to Roosevelt after the Williams-Ijams report of September 8, which absolved all concerned of any "negligence or mistaken judgment."[40] From Kennamer's reference to the reports of the American Legion, however, it is clear that their conclusions, based on a much more limited investigation than Kennamer was able to conduct, absolved the FERA and the Florida ERA of guilt in the matter.

In all of this, VA Administrator Hines played a curious role. Whatever his own views concerning FERA negligence in the deaths of the veterans, Hines was a team player, unwilling to embarrass President Roosevelt with the 1936 presidential election less than a year away. Thus, Hines busied himself early with "damage control" in the administration's relations with veterans groups as a result of the disaster. Two days after the hurricane, Hines huddled with White House aides Marvin McIntyre and Steve Early over the crisis and then hurried to meet the arrival of a train bearing the National Commander of the American Legion when it arrived in Washington at 11:30 P.M. There he conferred with the Legion official until 1:00 A.M. over Roosevelt's "wishes in the matter" and gained his cooperation.[41]

Similarly, Hines refused to make public the VA's views on the tragedy and its difference of opinion with the FERA. When Congresswoman Edith Nourse Rogers, ranking Republican member of the Committee on World War Veteran's Legislation, sought information from Hines on the disaster in the keys, she was referred instead to the Democratic chairman of the committee.[42] And in April and May 1936 Hines and Kennamer were silent concerning any possible negligence on the keys when they testified before a hearing of the House Committee on World War Veterans Legislation dealing with legislation for the relief of survivors of the disaster.[43]

Hines's own views in the matter seem clear, however, from his response to a memorandum he received from Under Secretary of the Interior Charles West in late March. In that memorandum, West had reviewed the reports of both the FERA and the VA, as well as those of the American Legion, and concluded: "It does not appear to the undersigned that the conclusions of the investigators for the Veteran's Administration are maintained by the record." Hines responded:

As a result of an investigation by representatives of the Federal Emergency Relief Administration and the Veterans' Administration, sworn testimony was secured from a large number of persons and important documentary evidence obtained, which, in my opinion, when considered in its entirety, does not sustain the conclusions contained in your memorandum.[44]

From this it seems clear that the VA administrator was as convinced as Ijams and Kennamer that negligence from the FERA in Washington down to the administrators in Florida had contributed to the tragedy in the keys.

In 1936 the veterans did receive their bonus. The bonus marchers of 1933-35, including over 250 who died in the Roosevelt administration's "rehabilitation" camps on the Florida Keys, slid once again into invisibility.

But the questions remain. As Ernest Hemingway wrote in his essay, "Who Murdered the Vets?":

Who sent nearly a thousand war veterans, many of them husky, hard-working and simply out of luck, but many of them close to the border of pathological cases, to live in frame shacks on the Florida Keys in hurricane months?

Why were the men not evacuated on Sunday, or, at latest, Monday morning, when it was known there was a possibility of a hurricane striking the Keys, and evacuation was their only possible protection?

Who advised against sending the train from Miami to evacuate the veterans until four-thirty o'clock on Monday so that it was blown off the tracks before it ever reached the lower camps?

These are questions that some one will have to answer, and answer satisfactorily, unless the clearing of Anacostia Flats is going to seem an act of kindness compared to the clearing of Upper and Lower Matecumbe.[45]

Notes

INTRODUCTION

1. Richard Kirkendall, "The New Deal and American Politics," Howard Sitkoff, ed., *Fifty Years Later: The New Deal Evaluated* (New York: McGraw, 1985), p. 14.

2. *Literary Digest*, 6-3-1933, p. 9.

3. Both newspapers are quoted in ibid.

4. Arthur Schlesinger, Jr., *The Coming of the New Deal* (New York: Houghton Mifflin, 1957), pp. 14-15.

5. Ernest Hemingway, quoted in *Literary Digest*, 9-28-1935, p. 7.

CHAPTER 1

1. D. W. Kennamer, "Report of Investigation of Florida Hurricane Disaster, October 30, 1935," Record Group 15, Subgroup 5-3, "Veterans Administration: Records of Investigation of Damage to Veterans' Camps Caused by the Hurricane of September 2, 1935," Washington National Records Center, Suitland, Maryland.

2. *Miami Daily News*, 10-18-1934.

3. F. C. Boyer, "Memorandum, December 20, 1934—Subject: Inspection of Veterans' Rehabilitation Camp, Islamorada, Florida," Record Group 69 006.1, Works Progress Administration:

Selected Records Relating to the 1935 Florida Hurricane, National Archives, Washington, D.C.

4. Joseph Hyde Pratt, "Report on the Veterans' Camps at Islamorada, Florida and Lower Matecumbe, Florida," 2-25-1935, RG 69 006.1.

5. Fred B. Ghent, "Report of Safety Inspection," 2-25-1935, RG 69 006.1.

6. Jerome A. Connor to B. M. Duncan, 2-26-1935, RG 69 006.1.

7. William P. Hogan and five other veterans to B. M. Duncan, 2-26-1935, RG 69 006.1.

8. *Miami Daily News*, 3-1-1935.

9. Ibid.

10. *Miami Daily News*, 3-25-1935.

11. Florida Emergency Relief Administration, "Expenditures on Veterans Program Monroe County, October 10, 1934 to April 30, 1935," RG 69 006.1.

12. Undated report of meeting held 3-2-1935, RG 69 006.1.

13. Joseph Hyde Pratt, memorandum of 3-5-1935, RG 69 006.1.

14. Statement of Conrad Van Hyning, undated, RG 69 006.1.

15. Edward T. Folliard, *Washington Post*, 3-24-1935.

16. Ibid., 3-25-1935.

17. "Strange Rehabilitation," editorial, *Washington Post*, 3-25-1935.

18. Julius F. Stone to B. M. Duncan, 3-16-1935, RG 69 006.1.

19. Statement of Lorin Scott, undated, RG 69 006.1.

20. Testimony of Conrad Van Hyning, 9-24-1935, RG 15, 5-3.

21. Statement of Albert G. Keith, undated, RG 69 006.1.

22. Fred B. Ghent to Joseph Hyde Pratt, 4-9-1935, RG 69 006.1.

23. Testimony of Fred B. Ghent, 9-19-1935, RG 15, 5-3.

24. Ibid.

25. Ibid.; according to Ghent's testimony this trip was made in early August.

26. Charles McLean, *New York Times*, 8-7-1935.

27. Ibid., 8-8-1935.

28. Ibid., 8-11-1935.

29. Ibid., 8-14-1935.

30. Raymond Clapper, *Washington Post*, 9-6-1935.

31. *New York Times*, 8-16-1935.

32. *Time*, 8-26-1935, p. 19.

33. Ibid., 9-16-1935, pp. 12-14.

34. Testimony of Fred B. Ghent, 9-19-1935, RG 15, 5-3.

CHAPTER 2

1. Statements of Walter J. Bennett, senior meteorologist, and Gordon E. Dunn, assistant forecaster, both of Jacksonville Weather Bureau, RG 69 006.1.

2. Testimony of G. S. Kennedy, meteorologist at Key West, 9-9-1935, RG 69 006.1.

3. Testimony of Ernest Carson, Miami Weather Bureau, 9-6-1935, RG 69 006.1.

4. Ibid.

5. Statement by Scott Loftin, 9-6-1935, RG 69 006.1.

6. Statement of J. L. Byrum, 10-1935, RG 69 006.1.

7. Statement of E. H. Hall, 9-10-1935, RG 69 006.1.

8. Statement of J. L. Byrum, 9-10-1935, RG 69 006.1.

9. Statement of Tony Lapinski, 9-19-1935, RG 69 006.1.

10. Statement of P. L. Gaddis, 9-10-1935, RG 69 006.1.

11. Ibid.

12. Statement by Scott Loftin, RG 69 006.1.

13. A. I. Pooser to C. L. Beale, general superintendent, FEC, 9-6-1935, RG 69 006.1.

14. Memorandum of telephone conversation between Lawrence Westbrook and Fred B. Ghent, RG 69 006.1.

15. Statement by Scott Loftin, RG 69 006.1.

16. William M. Johns, *Miami Daily News*, 9-5-1935.

17. Statement of William M. Johns, RG 69 006.1.

18. Statement of Ray W. Sheldon, 9-4-1935, RG 69 006.1.

19. Statement of W. N. Chambers, RG 69 006.1.

20. Statement of Martin M. Condry, RG 69 006.1.

21. Statement of John W. Fleming, RG 69 006.1.

22. Testimony of Mrs. L. A. Fritchman, RG 69 006.1.

23. Statement of John Good, RG 69 006.1.

24. Statement of Frederick Poock, RG 69 006.1.

25. Statement of Fred B. Ghent, RG 69 006.1.

26. Ibid.

27. Ibid.

28. Statement of William A. Hardaker, RG 69 006.1.
29. Testimony of E. H. Sheeran, RG 69 006.1.
30. Statement of Arthur Williams Mewshaw, 9-10-1935, RG 69 006.1.
31. Statement of Robert Aldrich Ayer, Jr., RG 69 006.1.
32. Statement of J. T. Wiggington, RG 69 006.1.
33. Testimony of Conrad Van Hyning, 9-24-1935, RG 69 006.1.
34. O. E. Hawk, field examiner, Veterans Administration, memorandum of interview by D. E. Kennamer with M. E. Gilfond, 9-27-1935, RG 69 006.1.
35. Testimony of Conrad Van Hyning, RG 69 006.1.
36. Ibid.
37. Memorandum signed by George W. Burke, 9-21-1935, RG 69 006.1.
38. Testimony of Captain Ed Butters, RG 69 006.1.
39. Statement of R. W. Craig, RG 69 006.1.
40. Statement of Rufus B. Johnson, RG 69 006.1.
41. Statement of John A. Russell, RG 69 006.1.
42. Statement of Albert S. Buck, RG 69 006.1.
43. Statement of Fred Bonner, Jr., RG 69 006.1.
44. Statement of D. A. Malcolm, RG 69 006.1.
45. Statement of F. L. Meyers, RG 69 006.1.
46. Statement of Eugene A. Pattison, RG 69 006.1.
47. Statement of O. D. Griffith, RG 69 006.1.
48. Interview with William M. Johns, RG 69 006.1.
49. Statement of Clyde Brannon, RG 69 006.1.
50. Statement of Lawrence J. O'Brien, RG 69 006.1.
51. Statement of Earle Roach, RG 69 006.1.
52. Statement of Arthur Ellis, RG 69 006.1.
53. Statement of Charles McClary, RG 69 006.1.
54. Statement of Ernest Belote, RG 69 006.1.
55. Statement of O. D. Griffith, RG 69 006.1.
56. Statement of William H. Klock, RG 69 006.1.
57. Statement of William Knox, RG 69 006.1.
58. Statement of B. M. Duncan, RG 69 006.1.
59. Testimony of E. H. Sheeran, RG 69 006.1.
60. Statement of Sam C. Cutler, RG 69 006.1.
61. Statement of John Good, RG 69 006.1.
62. Statement of O. D. Griffith, RG 69 006.1.
63. Testimony of Thomas Harrell, RG 69 006.1.

64. Statement of Mrs. L. A. Fritchmann, and of Albert S. Buck, RG 69 006.1.

65. Statement of Louis Maloney, RG 69 006.1.

66. Testimony of Fred B. Ghent, 9-7-1935, RG 69 006.1.

67. Testimony of Ray W. Sheldon, 9-7-1935, RG 69 006.1.

68. Statement of Eugene A. Pattison, RG 69 006.1.

69. Statement of Albert S. Buck, RG 69 006.1.

70. Statement of Joseph Hipolito Huau, RG 69 006.1.

71. Statements of E. A. Anderson, James Anderson, and W. D. Aycock, RG 69 006.1.

72. John F. Daniels to Veterans Administration, 3-15-1936, RG 69 006.1.

73. Statement of Frank R. Tischenbach, RG 69 006.1.

74. Statement of Herbert S. Wilshire, RG 69 006.1.

75. Statement of Joseph Wojtkiewicz, RG 69 006.1.

76. Statement of J. W. Taylor, RG 69 006.1.

77. Statement of Paul Pugh, RG 69 006.1.

78. Statement of George D. Barber, RG 69 006.1.

79. *Miami Herald*, 9-10-1935.

80. Statement of Terence Gormley, RG 69 006.1.

81. Testimony of C. C. Sain, RG 69 006.1.

82. Statement of E. H. Sheeran, 9-13-1935, RG 69 006.1.

83. Statement of Lloyd Everett, RG 69 006.1.

84. Statement of O. D. King, RG 69 006.1.

85. Statement of J. D. McLean, RG 69 006.1.

86. Statement of Ray Lester, RG 69 006.1.

87. Statement of Louis D. Kite, RG 69 006.1.

88. Statement of Wilbur E. Jones, RG 69 006.1.

89. Testimony of John Good, 9-17-1935, RG 15, 5-3.

90. Testimony of Samuel C. Cutler, 9-21-1935, RG 15, 5-3.

91. Statement of John Dombrauski, RG 69 006.1.

92. Statement of Harry Gaskins, RG 69 006.1.

93. Testimony of Eugene A. Pattison, RG 69 006.1.

94. Statement of Benjamin Myers, RG 69 006.1.

95. Testimony of W. Z. Burrus, 9-13-1935, RG 15, 5-3.

CHAPTER 3

1. Statement of J. R. Combs, RG 69 006.1.

2. Statement of Earle L. Fox, RG 69 006.1.

3. Statement of Gus Linawik, RG 69 006.1.

4. All of the preceding accounts were printed in the *Miami Daily News*, 9-4-1935.

5. Statement of Clyde Brannon, RG 69 006.1.

6. Statement of Jacob S. Herbert, RG 69 006.1.

7. Statements of Raleigh LePreux, one undated, one dated 9-23-1935, RG 69 006.1.

8. Statement of George Joseph Senison, 9-23-1935, RG 69 006.1.

9. Statement of William W. Terry, RG 69 006.1.

10. Written statement of Wilbur B. Cawthon, 9-16-1935, RG 69 006.1.

11. Statement of F. L. Meyer, RG 69 006.1.

12. *Miami Daiy News*, 9-5-1935.

13. Statement of B. E. Davis, 9-11-1935, RG 69 006.1.

14. Statement of Arthur Williams Mewshaw, 9-10-1935, RG 69 006.1.

15. Statement of Arthur Brown, 9-23-1935, RG 69 006.1.

16. Statement of Peter Donahue, RG 69 006.1.

17. Statement of Thomas F. Lannon, RG 69 006.1.

18. Statement of James Lennon, RG 69 006.1.

19. Statement of James B. Lindley, RG 69 006.1.

20. Statement of Gay Marion Postell, RG 69 006.1.

21. Statement of De Forest Rummage, 9-16-1935, RG 69 006.1.

22. These accounts are from the *Miami Daily News*, 9-5-1935.

23. Statement of Dexter V. Byers, RG 69 006.1.

24. Statement of William Kenneth Martin, RG 69 006.1.

25. Statement of Eugene C. Cunningham, RG 69 006.1.

26. Statement of Arbie Hytte, 9-21-1935, RG 69 006.1.

27. Statement of Gus Linnawak, RG 69 006.1.

CHAPTER 4

1. Henry Cavendish, *Miami Herald*, 9-5-1935.

2. *Literary Digest*, 9-14-1935, pp. 8-9.

3. *Time*, 9-16-1935, pp. 12-14.

4. *Newsweek*, 9-14-1935, p. 12.

5. Henry G. Frampton, *Miami Daily News*, 9-5-1935.

6. Jack Bell, *Miami Daily News*, 9-5-1935.

7. Ernest Hemingway, "Who Murdered the Vets?" *New Masses*, quoted in *Literary Digest*, 9-28-1935, p. 7.

8. Arthur Dunn, *Miami Daily News*, 9-9-1935.

9. Testimony of Major William V. Alburg, 9-27-1935, RG 15, 5-3.

10. *Miami Daiy News*, 9-6-1935.

11. Ibid.

12. Ibid., 9-7-1935.

13. Frank T. Hines to John E. Rankin, 5-4-1936, RG 15, 5-3.

14. *Miami Daily News*, 9-8-1935.

15. Editorial, *Miami Herald*, 9-8-1935.

16. *Miami Herald*, 9-9-1935.

17. *Miami Daily News*, 9-11-1935.

18. *Newsweek*, 9-14-1935.

CHAPTER 5

1. *Miami Daily News*, 9-6-1935.

2. Ibid.

3. Memo of telephone conversation between Col. Lawrence Westbrook and Fred B. Ghent, 9-5-1935, RG 69 006.1.

4. Telephone conversation between Col. Lawrence Westbrook and Marvin McIntyre, 9-4-1935, RG 69 006.1.

5. Telephone conversation between Col. Lawrence Westbrook and Julius F. Stone, 9-5-1935, RG 69 006.1.

6. Telephone conversation between Milford, Marvin Porter and Charles Forbes, 9-6-1935, RG 69 006.1.

7. "After the Tragedy," editorial, *Washington Post*, 9-7-1935.

8. Raymond Clapper, *Washington Post*, 9-6-1935.

9. Aubrey Williams and George Ijams, "Preliminary Report of Investigation of Key West Hurricane Disaster," 9-13-1935, RG 69 006.1.

10. Greater Miami Ministerial Association to Franklin D. Roosevelt, 9-10-1935, RG 69 006.1.

11. Reverend Frank A. Hamilton to Franklin D. Roosevelt, 9-11-1935, RG 69 006.1.

12. *Miami Herald*, 9-11-1935. The reference is to Paul "Blacky" Pugh of the camps.

13. *Miami Herald*, 9-11-1935.

14. Telephone conversation between Conrad Van Hyning and Aubrey Williams, 9-13-1935, RG 69 006.1.

15. *Miami Daily News*, 9-6-1935.

16. Ibid.

17. Ibid., 9-10-1935.

18. Ibid., 9-11-1935.

19. *New York Times*, 9-7-1935

20. Editorial, *Miami Herald*, 9-9-1935.

21. *Miami Herald*, 9-15-1935.

22. Ibid., 9-18-1935.

23. Ibid.

24. Ray Tucker, *Miami Daily News*, 9-17-1935.

25. *Miami Daily News*, 9-27-1935.

26. Telephone conversation between Aubrey Williams and John Abt, 9-14-1935, in RG 69 006.1.

27. D. W. Kennamer to Sam Jared, Jr., 9-12-1935, RG 15, 5-3.

28. D. W. Kennamer to Sam Jared, Jr., 9-15-1935, RG 15, 5-3.

29. Ibid.

30. Sam Jared, Jr., to D. W. Kennamer, 9-14-1935, RG 15, 5-3.

31. D. W. Kennamer, "Report of Investigation of Florida Hurricane Disaster," 10-30-1935, RG 15, 5-3.

32. For example, John Abt memorandum to Harry Hopkins, 1-10-1936, RG 15, 5-3.

33. A search of the Veterans Administration and Federal Emergency Relief Administration files, as well as the records in the Roosevelt Presidential Library, by the National Archives and Records Service in 1968 failed to find a copy of the Abt report and some other materials mentioned in correspondence. See memorandum from Director, Investigation and Service to Assistant Director of Investigation, 2-26-1968, RG 15, 5-3.

34. George E. Ijams to Frank T. Hines, 1-10-1936, RG 15, 5-3.

35. Frank T. Hines to Harry Hopkins, 2-5-1936, RG 15, 5-3. There is no evidence that this course of action was followed. See memorandum of 2-26-1968 cited above, RG 15, 5-3.

36. D. W. Kennamer, memorandum with "General Comment" attached, 6-23-1936, RG 15, 5-3.

37. Ray Murphy to Franklin D. Roosevelt, 11-2-1935, RG 69 006.1.

38. Franklin D. Roosevelt, memorandum to Harry Hopkins, 11-6-1935, RG 69 006.1.

39. Frank T. Hines to Harry Hopkins, 11-16-1935, RG 69 006.1.

40. See memorandum of 2-26-1968 cited above, in RG 15, 5-3.

41. Frank T. Hines to Marvin McIntyre, 9-5-1935, RG 15, 5-3.

42. Edith Nourse Rogers to Frank T. Hines, 2-24-1936, RG 15, 5-3.

43. U.S. Congress, House, *Florida Hurricane Disaster: Hearings Before the Committee on World War Veterans Legislation,* 74th Congress, 2nd session, HR 9486, 1936, passim.

44. Frank T. Hines to Charles West, 3-31-1936, RG 15, 5-3.

45. Ernst Hemingway, "Who Murdered the Vets?" *New Masses,* quoted in *Literary Digest,* 9-28-1935, p. 7.

Bibliographic Essay

Materials concerning the tragedy can be found in two record groups of the National Archives and Records Administration. Record Group 69 006.1 of the National Archives contains the Federal Emergency Relief Administration documents relating to the hurricane, while Record Group 15, 5-3, of the Washington National Records Center contains the Veterans Administration files. Investigations by these two agencies reached very different conclusions concerning the culpability of the officials responsible for the safety of the veterans and both record groups must be consulted to get a reasonably complete picture of the circumstances in the camps that weekend.

As pointed out in the introduction, histories of the New Deal and biographies of Franklin Delano Roosevelt are of no assistance in uncovering information about this incident. Arthur Schlesinger, *The Coming of the New Deal* (New York: Houghton Mifflin, 1957), is nevertheless interesting for its description of Roosevelt's treatment of the bonus marchers in Washington during the early months of his administration and for the unfair comparisons he makes with the Hoover administration.

Both the *Miami Herald* and the *Miami Daily News* are useful not only for their accounts of the conditions surrounding the hurricane, but also for their descriptions of the camps in the months preceding it. The *Washington Post* articles (March 24 and 25, 1935) describing conditions in the camps are most useful, as are those in the *New York Times* August 1935 editions cited in the notes. Good descriptions of the damage wrought by the hurricane can be found in *Literary Digest*, September 14 and 28, 1935; *Newsweek*, September 14, 1935; and *Time*, September 16, 1935.

Index

ABOUT THE AUTHOR

GARY DEAN BEST is Professor of History at the University of Hawaii at Hilo. He is the author of *The Politics of American Individualism* (Greenwood, 1975), *To Free a People* (Greenwood, 1982), *Herbert Hoover: The Postpresidential Years* (2 volumes, 1983), and *Pride, Prejudice, and Politics: Roosevelt versus Recovery, 1933-1938* (Praeger, 1991), as well as numerous essays for scholarly books and journals. He has held fellowships from the American Historical Association and the National Endowment for the Humanities and was a Fulbright Scholar in Japan from 1974 to 1975.